HEEEEEEEEEY!!!!!!!!!

I'm Just a "Sista" Tryin' to Tell Somebody about JESUS!

HEEEEEEEEEY!!!!!!!!!!
I'm Just a "Sista" Tryin' to Tell Somebody about JESUS!

by
Wilma L. McGee

LOWBAR
PUBLISHING COMPANY

905 South Douglas Avenue • Nashville, Tennessee 37204
Phone: 615-972-2842
E-mail: Lowbarpublishingcompany@gmail.com
Web site: www.Lowbarbookstore.com

Nashville, Tennessee
Printed in the United States of America in 2014.

ISBN: 978-0-9886237-4-3
Lowbar Publishing Company
Nashville, Tennessee 37204
615-972-2842
E-mail: Lowbarpublishingcompany@gmail.com
Web site: www.Lowbarbookstore.com

For additional information, workshop, and seminars, here is how you may contact the author:

Wilma L. McGee
P.O. Box 456
Hazel Park, Michigan 48030-0456
Phone: 313-770-0458
E-mail: babydoll1948@sbcglobal.net
Copy Editor: Honey B. Higgins
Graphic and Cover Design Artist: Norah S. Branch

Scripture references in this book are taken from the *King James Version* of the Holy Bible, unless otherwise noted.

All rights reserved under the International Copyright Law. Contents and/or cover may not be reproduced in whole or in part in any form without the expressed written consent of the author or publisher.

Copyright © 2014

TABLE OF CONTENTS

Foreword		vii
Introduction		1
Chapter		
1	In the Beginning…	3
2	Destruction and Restoration	8
3	Instruction: The Ten Commandments	11
4	JESUS	24
5	Faith	29
6	Teachers—Teaching Prayer	32
7	Teachers—Teaching Love	37
8	Teachers—Teaching about Giving	42
9	Teachers: Men and Women	48
10	Teachers—Teaching Behavior	53
11	Teachers—Teaching about Marriage	60
12	Conclusion	63
	About the Author	65

Foreword

As Christians, we are mandated to tell the Gospel story—the Good News regarding Jesus Christ. We need to let others know, particularly the unsaved, what Jesus has done for us. We need to tell as many people as we can about God's love—about His salvation through His Son, Jesus Christ.

> *"But you shall receive power when the Holy Spirit has come upon you; and you shall be witnesses to Me in Jerusalem, and in all Judea and Samaria, and to the end of the earth" (Acts 1:8, NKJV).*

> *"And He said to them, 'Go into all the world and preach the gospel to every creature'" (Mark 16:15, NKJV).*

If there was ever a time when people needed to hear the Gospel of Jesus Christ, that time is now!

Wilma McGee is one of those faithful saints who lovingly tells others about the Savior. She is a determined and devoted witness of Jesus Christ. This book is the pouring out of her heart and soul to encourage believers to be witnesses of Him.

In our modern, technologically advanced world, we are constantly being bombarded with messages of all kinds—messages that *sell* (drive this car and feel powerful; use this cologne and the ladies will go crazy for you; wear these clothes and you'll make a great impression on everyone you meet), and messages that *tell* ("Did you hear what happened to Joe yesterday?" "Karen got that job she so desperately wanted." "Today's lesson is on the rise of the Civil Rights Movement in America." "My feet hurt!").

This barrage of messages is delivered in a variety of ways: through television commercials, radio ads, Facebook posts, text messages, classroom lectures, barber shop chats, beauty salon discussions, movies, books, and magazines, over pulpits, and on iPads, iPods, and iPhones.

Through the maddening maze of messages, we need to hear words of hope, expressions of peace, and the Good News of salvation. Thank God for the faithful witnesses who are trying to tell somebody about Jesus! Thank God for Wilma, who is just a "sista" tryin' to tell somebody about Jesus!

In this book, Wilma writes from the heart to convey to us principles and commandments of Scripture that compel us to spread the Gospel and to live the Gospel. Chapter after chapter, Wilma inspires Christians to both share the Gospel and to live their lives according to the Word of God. It is not only our words, but also our deeds that speak loudly and clearly in our witness for Jesus. We are to speak boldly for Jesus and to let our lights so shine before men that they see our good works and glorify our Father in heaven.

Her style is what I call "straight up, no chaser"—as she uses the Word of God in an unadulterated fashion to communicate her points. For the most part, she lets the Bible do the talking. This book is clear in its purpose: to convict the readers to have a relationship with God if they do not already have one…and if they do, to have a better one.

Wilma and her husband, the Reverend Herman McGee, are akin to Aquila and Priscilla of the early church, a couple devoted to God and to one another. They are partners in ministry and in life. I had the privilege and honor of presiding over their wedding and they are more in love today than they were then—over fourteen years, five months, two weeks, four days, eighteen hours, and thirty-five minutes ago (as of the time of this writing)! They are a joy to know and a pleasure to work with!

Thank you, Wilma, for writing this book and sharing your thoughts with us. Through this book, I am inspired to be a better "brotha" tryin' to tell somebody about Jesus!

Peace and Blessings,
Rev. Patrick O. Lindsey

Rev. Lindsey is the Pastor of Greater Bibleway Missionary Baptist Church in Detroit, Michigan, and Vice President of Government and Community Affairs at Wayne State University in Detroit, Michigan.

INTRODUCTION

This writing began in December of 2009 because the lyrics to a particular song—"I'm just a nobody, trying to tell everybody, about Somebody, who can save anybody"—came to mind. I thought of how I desire so much to witness for our Lord and Savior Jesus Christ and tell others about the goodness of God, His Father—to tell them about His life, His birth, His death, His burial, and His resurrection; to tell them about how He only wants obedience and praise from us, we who have the choice to become His: Jesus' brothers and sisters... God's children. John 1:12 attests to this: "But as many as received him, to them gave he power to become the sons of God, even to them that believe on his name" (KJV). I desire to tell others that when one makes the decision not to follow Christ, he or she is destroyed; this is made evident in Hosea 4:6: "My people are destroyed for lack of knowledge: because thou hast rejected knowledge, I will also reject thee, that thou shalt be no priest to me: seeing thou hast forgotten the law of thy God, I will also forget thy children."

I can appreciate the writer of the aforementioned song saying that "he [is] just a nobody," perhaps meaning that he carries no high position or title; that he is just a mere man who has a relationship with the Lord and wants to tell all he can about Jesus. I, too, want to tell it; however, I choose to say that I am *somebody*—for I carry the title of "a child of the King," a royal priesthood, a child of God; I am a sister to His only begotten Son, and I am trying to tell all I can about JESUS to whomever will listen!

In reading this text I have written, one will find that the content is based on the Word of God and is applicable for our daily living. It is a must that I tell others about Jesus because of the instructions found in Matthew 28:18-20. We are taught that those Scripture verses comprise the Great Commission, and I feel compelled to be obedient to that call: "And Jesus came and spake unto them, saying, All power is given unto me in heaven and in earth. Go ye therefore, and teach all nations, baptizing them in the name of the Father, and of the Son, and of the Holy Ghost: Teaching them to observe all things whatsoever I have commanded you: and, lo, I am with you alway, even unto the end of the world. Amen."

What an honor! God has entrusted us to spread His Holy Word to the people of the world. How wonderfully blessed we are (or can be) by living according to His Word. I believe that this is my commission: to spread and live His Word not only in this writing but in my daily walk and talk with Him. I am commissioned to live, as well as committed to living, His Word. It is my desire that the readers of this writing will be blessed according to God's Word. It is my prayer that those who do not have a relationship with God will be inspired to seek Him, and that those who have a relationship with Him will also be inspired—for 2 Timothy 2:15 asserts the following: "Study to shew thyself approved unto God, a workman that needeth not to be ashamed, rightly dividing the word of truth."

I say to my readers, "May God forever bless you as you go forth."

Chapter 1

In the Beginning...

It all started...hmm... some years ago (well over two thousand, actually)—because *it is written* in the Holy Scriptures that "In the beginning God..." (Genesis 1:1), and "In the beginning was the Word, and the Word was with God, and the Word was God" (John 1:1). Now, some people have written that the Word was "a god." This is rather unfortunate, because it is also written in the Holy Scriptures that God's people are destroyed for lack of knowledge: "*My* people are destroyed for lack of knowledge: because thou hast rejected knowledge, I will also reject thee, that thou shalt be no priest to me: seeing thou hast forgotten the law of thy God, I will also forget thy children" (Hosea 4:6). We have the Word of God at our fingertips and yet choose to act in ways that oppose His will—knowing that He exists. "*The heavens declare* the glory of God; and the firmament sheweth his handiwork" (Psalm 19:1). How could anyone ever deny His existence when we see the Earth, the sky, life itself?

~Hey, I'm just a "sista" tryin' to tell somebody about JESUS.~

In the beginning was the Word, and the Word was with God, and the Word was God. The same was in the beginning with God. All things were made by him; and without him was not any thing made that was made. In him was life; and the life was the light of men. And the light shineth in darkness; and the darkness comprehended it not. There was a man sent from God, whose name was John. The same came for a witness, to bear witness of the Light, that all men through him might believe. He was not that Light, but was sent to bear witness of that Light. That was the true Light, which lighteth every man that cometh into the world. He was in the world, and the world was made by him, and the world knew him not. *(Imagine that—the world knew Him not. Do you know Him?)* He came unto his own, and his own received him not. *(Can you imagine going around your family and they not know you or even want you in their presence?)* But as many as received him, to them gave he power to become the sons of God *(He made us His brothers and sisters)*, even to them that believe on his name: Which were born, not of blood, nor of the will of the flesh, nor of the will of man, but of God ***(not the blood that flows through our bodies; but a spiritual birth)***. And the Word *(JESUS)* was made flesh, and dwelt among us, (and we beheld his glory, the glory as of the only begotten of the Father,) full of grace and truth. (John 1:1-14)

As affirmed by the previous Scripture text, the Word is Jesus Himself. He is the Son of God, in whom we live, move, and have our being—Jesus, the Word, the one who died for our sins; the one who made it possible for us to be alive, both in the flesh and spiritually.

In the beginning, God had great plans for us as He created the heaven and the Earth. He created everything for man. He created man (see Genesis 1:26-27), who had it made. He, God, created day and night, light and darkness, and the sun and the moon and the stars. He created rivers of waters. He created the dry land. He created grass, herb-yielding seed, and the fruit tree that yields fruit. He created life in the waters (i.e., fish, whales); He created the fowl that fly above the Earth. God spoke and the Earth brought forth cattle and living creatures after His kind. God created all that man could need—then He created man: in His image and in His likeness, without sin, being good and very good. He took man and put him in the Garden of Eden to dress it and keep it (to maintain and cultivate it).

"And God blessed them, and God said unto them, Be fruitful, and multiply, and replenish the earth, and subdue it: and have dominion over the fish of the sea, and over the fowl of the air, and over every living thing that moveth upon the earth" (Genesis 1:28). From the beginning, obedience was a part of God's plan for humanity's living in the physical and in the spiritual. God gave instructions to man and in giving these instructions, He pointed out to man specifically the trees that he could eat from…and the tree that he should not eat of. In creating man, God gave him a work to do, but also allowed him to eat of the fruit of his labor. He gave the command to Adam, the command that initiated obedience (see Genesis 2:15-17). But as we learn in later Scripture, man disobeyed and man fell (see Genesis 3).

In the beginning, Satan had his part to play as well. At one time, Satan was an angel—but because of disobedience, because of the desires of his heart, he was cast out of heaven.

> How art thou fallen from heaven, O Lucifer, son of the morning! how art thou cut down to the ground, which didst weaken the nations! For thou hast said in thine heart, I will ascend into heaven, I will exalt my throne above the stars of God: I will sit also upon the mount of the congregation, in the sides of the north: I will ascend above the heights of the clouds: I will be like the most High. Yet thou shalt be brought down to hell, to the sides of the pit. (Isaiah 14:12-15)

> He had waged a war in heaven…and he lost.

> And there was war in heaven: Michael and his angels fought against the dragon; and the dragon fought and his angels, And prevailed not; neither was their place found any more in heaven. And the great dragon was cast out, that old serpent, called the Devil, and Satan, which deceiveth the whole world: he was cast out into the earth, and his angels were cast out with him. (Revelation 12:7-9)

Can you imagine that: Satan having a battle in heaven—with God? He tried to take over in God's territory and *lost*. (There is *a life lesson to be learned* from this: One should never go to someone else's home to fight—for he or she has no idea what or who he or she is up against.) As a result, Satan, in his anger, has been warring ever since. So seeing as though he himself cannot get to God, he tries to do so through God's children—us. And what parent would allow anyone to bother his children? God is even better than our parents when it comes to protecting us, His children.

At every opportunity, Satan gets busy. His first attempt was in the Garden of Eden, the place where God took Adam after He created him. He also created Eve. God put Adam to sleep. Some theologians say that God performed the first "transplant" surgery when He took one of Adam's ribs and made woman (see Genesis 2:21-23). God created the woman and brought her to Adam, whom then called her "woman" because she was taken out of man. That would qualify that "women are God's gifts to men." Special? I say yes!

~Hey, I'm just a "sista" tryin' to tell somebody about JESUS.~

In the beginning…man fell. Why? God created everything that man needed and gave him instructions—God's commands. So everybody must have known the rules of order, right? In that case, there should not have been any problems…except for the fact that that dirty rascal, that dirty fighter, that old devil—Satan—got busy.

Why is it that the strong prey on the weak? He, Satan, went to the woman, probably smooth talking her, saying all that she wanted to hear; she then got comfortable with what he was saying and let down her guard. Where was Adam when Satan came for a visit? And the "woman"—shouldn't she have felt the need to inquire the counsel of her husband before listening to Satan? But, alas, she acted of her own "free will." In Genesis 3, there is evidence of Satan being a smooth operator in his accomplishing his goal with the fall of man. He presented such an invitation to knowing the difference between good and evil that the "woman" could not resist. After all, who, if it sounds or looks good, does not want all of it? Remember Hosea 4:6. In his curiosity, man fell into sin—doomed to eternal damnation in the fires of hell—because of disobedience.

In the beginning…was the start to there being consequences for decisions made: (1) the "woman" would experience pain, suffering, and sorrow in child bearing, as well as having to show obedience to her "own" husband. Some try to blame the "woman" for the Fall; however, what happened when she ate of the Tree of the Knowledge of Good and Evil? Nothing! BUT…she gave it to her husband, persuaded him to eat, and their eyes were then opened (see Genesis 3:6-7); so, (2) this was the consequence for the man: "Unto Adam [God] said, Because thou hast hearkened unto the voice of thy wife, and hast eaten of the tree, of which I commanded thee, saying, Thou shalt not eat of it: cursed is the ground for thy sake; in sorrow shalt thou eat of it all the days of thy life." Husbands…WOW!

Isn't it something how when we do wrong, our eyes are opened even today? We are exposed and guilt sets in. We try to hide and cover up; but, God knows and sees all. In the beginning…

~Hey, I'm just a "sista" tryin' to tell somebody about JESUS.~

Chapter 2

Destruction and Restoration

My people are destroyed for lack of knowledge: because thou hast rejected knowledge, I will also reject thee, that thou shalt be no priest to me: seeing thou hast forgotten the law of thy God, I will also forget thy children.—Hosea 4:6

That Scripture reference just keeps popping up, doesn't it? Man showed such defiance toward God (like children sometimes do to their own parents) that discipline became necessary. Man was so out of control that God, in His infinite wisdom, chose to destroy man—His creation. Man became so wicked that it grieved God that He had made man. It was once said by a preacher, "God realized that He had made a mistake when He created man"; however, the fact is that God does not make mistakes. Thus, He knew before we were ever created what would happen and had a Plan of Salvation already lying in wait.

~Hey, I'm just a "sista" tryin' to tell somebody about JESUS.~

Hundreds of years passed between the time of Adam and the time of Noah, who was a man who found grace in the eyes of the Lord. God chose Noah to be the new beginning after man's destruction. Noah was five hundred-plus years of age when God instructed him to make the ark. It was an ark of deliverance—as would soon be discovered. When it came time for the rain, Noah was six hundred years old. WOW! He spent approximately one hundred years making the ark.

Let us take a look at Noah's character, and his walk with God. In learning about Noah's character, we discover these things: he walked with God—"Noah found grace in the eyes of the LORD. These are the generations of Noah: Noah was a just man and perfect in his generations, and Noah walked with God" (Genesis 6:8-9); and he was obedient—"Noah did according unto all that the LORD commanded him" (Genesis 7:5).

As in the previous Scripture writings, we learn that God had given instructions to man (in the Garden of Eden); but, man fell, and in his falling (the result of having free will), he decided to do things his way instead of God's way: "And God looked upon the earth, and, behold, it was corrupt; for all flesh had corrupted his way upon the earth" (Genesis 6:12). It is so amazing how when we make these decisions against God's will, we "monk' up" things ("monk'," in this context, was one of my father's frequent sayings for making an error—which was a shortened version of "monkeying around"); we do not want to admit to our wrongness so we keep trying to fix things, which puts us on a continual downward spiral.

In Noah's case, he truly believed in God and walked with Him, listened to Him, and followed His instructions—he was the essence of obedience—as is seen in the following verses: "Thus did Noah; according to all that God commanded him, so did he" (Genesis 6:22); "And the LORD said unto Noah, Come thou and all thy house into the ark; for thee have I seen righteous before me in this generation" (Genesis 7:1). God, in His divine wisdom, brought salvation to Noah and his house because of Noah's obedience. That is all that is required of us when we accept Jesus as Lord and Savior of our lives—obedience to His Word. When we obey His Word, we are acting in accordance to His will.

After the destruction of all mankind and all on the Earth, because of Noah's obedience, God blessed him and his sons and told them to be fruitful and multiply and replenish the Earth. (*Obedience*: "the condition or quality of being obedient; complying or submissive to authority.")

Another notable aspect of Noah's life is the fact that after God spared him and his family in the Flood, Noah offered a sacrifice unto God, which was one of the intended purposes for having the clean animals on the ark. (Sacrifices of clean animals were done during that time for the atonement of sin.) "And Noah built an altar unto the LORD; and took of every clean beast, and of every clean fowl, and offered burnt offerings on the altar" (Genesis 8:20). It was at that point in time that God entered into the Noahic covenant:

> And the LORD smelled a sweet savour; and the LORD said in his heart, I will not again curse the ground any more for man's sake; for the imagination of man's heart is evil from his youth; neither will I again smite any more every thing living, as I have done. While the earth remaineth, seedtime and harvest, and cold and heat, and summer and winter, and day and night shall not cease. (Genesis 8:21-22)

We obey those in positions of authority on our jobs, in school, in our families, and so forth—yet we, for whatever the reason, seem to have difficulty with obeying God. Is it because His Word is written, though we cannot see Him? He talks to us: at times when one voice tells us to do something wrong and then another says "no," that is GOD. Because we think we know the outcome, we listen to the negative forces—Satan. But God wants our obedience to Him, no matter what. What about those choices that we make? I have heard it said that "the choices we make dictate the life that we live." How true a statement! We know right from wrong but, so often, we choose to do wrong because of the desires of the flesh. Rev. Herman McGee, my husband, often says, "Everything that God created is still doing what it is supposed to do—except man. The dogs are still barking, the birds are still singing, the cows are still mooing, and the trees are still growing. But, man!" God commands obedience: "And Samuel said, Hath the LORD as great delight in burnt offerings and sacrifices, *as in obeying the voice of the* LORD? Behold, *to obey is better than sacrifice*, and to hearken than the fat of rams" (2 Samuel 15:22). Hold on! *No* God, *no* peace; *know* God, *know* peace. Obey HIM!

~Hey, I'm just a "sista" tryin' to tell somebody about JESUS.~

Chapter 3

Instruction: The Ten Commandments

Take my yoke upon you, and learn of me; for I am meek and lowly in heart: and ye shall find rest unto your souls.—Matthew 11:29

(While this is a lengthy chapter, it is so vital to characterizing our walks with God.)

Some two thousand-plus years had passed from the time of Noah to that of Moses—and within that period of time, man fell (and continues to fall today). He makes decisions as Lucifer did (when he was kicked out of heaven), who just keeps trying even today to make himself equal to God or to be better than God. This next section is a breakdown of the Ten Commandments. (Refer to Exodus 20:3-17.) (Be mindful that anyone who has broken one of these commandments—though maybe has not committed any of the others—is still guilty of breaking "the *law* of all the commandments." Case in point: while there are many laws in this world, even when just one of them has been broken, the "law" has been broken.

1) Thou shalt have no other gods before me (verse 3). "Give unto the Lord the glory due unto his name: bring an offering, and come before him: worship the Lord in the beauty of holiness" (1 Chronicles 16:29). What is it that keeps us from serving God? Is it our family and friends that keep us from serving God in the beauty of holiness? We get so sidetracked by the "What about me?" mentality that we forget the very reason why we *are*: it is because of God. It is He who hath made us and not we ourselves. We forget about Him until something happens, which oftentimes is something drastic. We should come to Him first and let Him lead and guide us in the way that we should go.

We should put nothing before God—as He is a jealous God. "Thou shalt not bow down thyself to them, nor serve them: *for I the* LORD *thy God am a jealous God,* visiting the iniquity of the fathers upon the children unto the third and fourth generation of them that hate me" (Exodus 20:5). He does not want us putting anything or anybody before HIM. Not husbands, wives, children, houses, jobs, finances. We need to assess and take inventory of those things that we are focusing on more than God and shift the focus to God. We need to examine ourselves: "But seek ye first the kingdom of God, and his righteousness; and all these things shall be added unto you" (Matthew 6:33). When God sees in our hearts that our love is for Him, He reacts in order to supply our need according to His riches in glory by Christ Jesus (see Philippians 4:19). When we seek Him first, everything that we need comes to us in great supply.

2) Thou shalt not make unto thee any graven image, or any likeness of any thing that is in heaven above, or that is in the earth beneath, or that is in the water under the earth (verse 4). Wow! God has so blessed man in his abilities to advance technologically that he sees himself as a god. Laptops, iPods and iPads, cell phones, wood carvings, markings on our bodies—all these are things that "we can't seem to get along without." They have become our "daily life." It is like we cannot begin the day without them. Whatever happened to the days when there were no cell phones, no answering machines, and no computers? It is like man cannot live without modern technology today. Everywhere we go, male and female, old and young are holding on to something in their hands to the point that they are not even paying attention to where they are going. Case in point: a woman was crossing a parking lot; I saw her but she did not see me for focusing on the instrument in her hand. I stopped. She walked into my vehicle. It could have been her life.

As another example, at one time, tattoos were very rare—so rare, in fact, that one had to be up close to a person bearing one in order to see what it was. Now tattoos can be spotted from a mile away, because there are some individuals who have covered their bodies completely in them. How sad. "Ye shall not make any cuttings in your flesh for the dead, nor print any marks upon you: I am the LORD" (Leviticus 19:28). We have made the dead a god by putting "r.i.p. (whoever)" on our arms and/or across our backsides... and for what reason(s)? For the sake of being noticed (because it does, in fact, draw attention). I know—it is a fad thing, right? Why not make it a fad to live right? Why not make it a fad to be obedient to the Word of God? Believers should set their own trend of doing what is right in God's sight.

~Hey, I'm just a "sista" tryin' to tell somebody about JESUS.~

3) Thou shalt not take the name of the LORD thy God in vain; for the LORD will not hold him guiltless that taketh his name in vain (verse 7). These days, it seems as though a conversation cannot be held without saying God's name and a foul word in the same sentence. Where is the respect for God? Where is our respect for each other? The language today seems to be limited to three-, four-, five-, and twelve-letter words before a point can be made. This kind of talk has become acceptable in the business place, in our homes, and, sadly, in our churches—the house of God, the place of worship. And most people think nothing of it. We call each other names that God never intended for us to call each other. Our tongues are as the Scriptures describe: *an unruly evil*; this point is expounded upon in the following verses: "But the tongue can no man tame; it is an unruly evil, full of deadly poison. Therewith bless we God, even the Father; and therewith curse we men, which are made after the similitude of God. Out of the same mouth proceedeth blessing and cursing. My brethren, these things ought not so to be" (James 3:8-9). While driving down the freeway one day during heavy traffic hours, I saw this billboard that read, "Keep using my name in vain and I'll make rush hour longer!....GOD." That was just so funny to me! (Praise God that I have learned to either not take the freeway if I am in a hurry, or to just be patient in my waiting.) Instead of profaning the name of God (or being profane, period), we should ponder this: "Finally, brethren, whatsoever things are true, whatsoever things are honest, whatsoever things are just, whatsoever things are pure, whatsoever things are lovely, whatsoever things are of good report;

if there be any virtue, and if there be any praise, think on these things" (Philippians 4:8).

We need to remember that when we are talking or having heated discussions, as Christians, our language needs to reflect Christianity, particularly when we are around children; they learn from what they hear and see, and those words will come back to haunt us when we least expect it. There are plenty of advertisements for products and/or services to aid people in learning other languages; however, I do not think that this is what God had in mind for Christians who should use different speech or words: "And thou shalt love the LORD thy God with all thine heart, and with all thy soul, and with all thy might. And *these words*, which I command thee this day, shall be in thine heart: And thou shalt teach them diligently unto thy children, and shalt talk of them when thou sittest in thine house, and when thou walkest by the way, and when thou liest down, and when thou risest up" (Deuteronomy 6:5-7).

Here are some "love" and/or "peace" sentiments uttered in other languages: **Te Amo** ("I love you" in Latin); or, **Assalamu alaikum** ("Peace be upon you" [Islamic]); and, **Mele Kalikimaka** ("Merry Christmas" in the Hawaiian language"). As with these sentiments, we must speak in a language that becomes holiness—after all, believers are a holy people, because God made us in His image and likeness; and He tells us this: "But as he which hath called you is *holy*, so *be ye holy* in all manner of conversation (your speech and the way you live); Because it is written, *Be ye holy*; for I am *holy*" (1 Peter 1:15-16).

~Hey, I'm just a "sista" tryin' to tell somebody about JESUS.~

4) Remember the Sabbath day, to keep it holy (verse 8). In Christ, Sunday is considered some Christians' Sabbath day, because we are taught that Jesus was risen from the dead on that day—so this is the day that some Christians go to church to worship Him, the day observed by most Christians in commemoration of the resurrection of Christ. *Sabbath* means "the seventh day of the week"; yet, Saturday is the day of rest and religious observance among the Jews and some Christians. "For in six days the LORD made heaven and earth, the sea, and all that in them is, and rested the seventh day: wherefore the LORD blessed the sabbath day, and hallowed it" (Exodus 20:11). In the beginning, God created the heavens and the Earth and all that is therein in six days—and on the seventh day He rested. So going fishing, washing the car, mowing the lawn, doing the laundry, and so forth, are not to be done on the Sabbath. Go to someone's church who is teaching Jesus' birth, death, burial, and resurrection; we must let God be our God.

~Hey, I'm just a "sista" tryin' to tell somebody about JESUS.~

5) Honor thy father and thy mother: that thy days may be long upon the land which the LORD thy God giveth thee (verse 12). This is the only commandment with a promise. Any idea of how a person may be able to live a long life? The answer is found in this fifth commandment: we must honor our fathers and mothers, "that [our] days may be long upon the land which the LORD [our] God [has given us]." And just an FYI: This would apply not just to our earthly mothers and fathers, but to our senior mothers and fathers in the faith as well. We must have respect for them all; we must not say and do just any old thing around them. For starters, the proper way to address them is by saying "Yes, ma'am" and "No, ma'am," and "Yes, sir" and "No, sir"—not "Yeah" and "Uh huh." The elderly deserve and should be shown respect: "Rebuke not an elder, but intreat him as a father; ... The elder women as mothers" (1 Timothy 5:1, 2a); "The glory of young men is their strength: and the beauty of old men is the gray head" (Proverbs 20:29).

Younger persons must have respect for the position of elders. They are older; thus, their status should warrant them the courtesy of being offered a seat in a crowded room. And in talking to them, it is unacceptable to converse with them with the intent of belittling them. Those of us who are caregivers for elderly persons must be kind to them, treating them the way we would like to be treated. Remember the saying, "What goes around comes around"? It is a very true sentiment: "Be not deceived; God is not mocked: for whatsoever a man soweth, that shall he also reap" (Galatians 6:7).

6) Thou shalt not kill (verse 13). We must not kill each other. The word *kill*, according to *The American Heritage Dictionary* (Second College Edition), means "to deprive of life; to put an end to; extinguish; to destroy a vitally essential quality in"; to deprive of life ("in any manner"; refer to another dictionary for these words)—*any manner*. This could mean doing so via shooting, stabbing, poisoning, drunk driving, setting on fire, drowning…and many other ways! Thou shalt not kill! Killing is the act of one individual making the decision to take the life of another. None of us can *give* life; therefore, we are not to *take* a life. Someone who makes the decision to kill—to end the life of another—is basically trying to act as God: the giver of life. God is the only one who can make such a decision. Anyone who makes the decision to take a life will dearly suffer the consequences. Let's remember Cain and Abel. Cain was so jealous of his brother, Abel, that he killed him. I would imagine that he suffered the punishment placed upon him (for that act) in such a way that he himself wanted to die. He became a vagabond—an idle wanderer without a permanent home or visible means of support.

Now we will assess being told that "Thou shalt not kill" while at the same time being told that there is "a time to kill." Many have asked, "How can God say, 'Thou shalt not kill' on one hand and on the other say that there is 'a time to kill'?" The latter is mentioned in the book of Ecclesiastes: "To every thing there is a season, and a time to every purpose under the heaven: … A time to kill, and a time to heal; a time to break down, and a time to build up" (3:1, 3). Some have highlighted these particular Scriptures to suggest that God's Word contradicts itself. To understand God's stance, we have to look at the reasoning behind both statements. When we are told, "Thou shalt not kill," this means that we are not to kill willfully, "just because," or on a dare. However, God's asserting that there is "a time to kill" is in reference to one's engaging in self-defense, protecting himself or herself or his or her family, and so forth: "And I looked, and rose up, and said unto the nobles, and to the rulers, and to the rest of the people, Be not ye afraid of them: remember the Lord, which is great and terrible, *and fight for your brethren, your sons, and your daughters, your wives, and your houses*" (Nehemiah 4:14).

This is not to say that an individual may purposely set out to kill; it simply means that we are permitted to protect our families and that which belongs to us—and that if in the midst of our protecting ourselves, our families, or our property we happen to cause the death of another, this is considered self-defense. When we make the choice to take the life of another for reasons other than self-defense, that is where God's law comes in: *Thou shalt not kill.* In today's legal system, the decision is made by a jury of peers as to whether an individual who has murdered another was justified in doing so.

The act of killing is not always accomplished through violent means. Sometimes we can speak and life is gone from the other person (as in an incident of killing with unkind words), or sometimes we can do things that may cause another person to die in his or her spirit. In today's society, bullying contributes to the deaths of many youth (either through homicide or suicide). Our words should be words of encouragement—words that help others in their growth. Our deeds should be acts of kindness—helping to build others up, not to tear them down.

Remember the rhyme uttered in childhood: "Sticks and stones may break my bones, but words will never hurt me"? Well, while words may not cause physical harm, unkind words can cut deep into the emotions of another, tearing him or her apart emotionally and mentally because of his or her worry over what others say about him or her, or how others feel about him or her. This sentiment is addressed in James 3:8-10: "But the tongue can no man tame; it is an unruly evil, full of deadly poison. Therewith bless we God, even the Father; and therewith curse we men, which are made after the similitude of God. Out of the same mouth proceedeth blessing and cursing. My brethren, these things ought not so to be." We should always think before we speak, constantly asking ourselves this question: Is what I am about to say necessary?

Even though what we are about to say to or about someone may be true, we must ponder and keep in mind these two questions: What do I expect to accomplish by saying what I am about to say? Will it construct or destruct? We are to love and encourage each other. It has been said that there are four things that we can never get back in life: the opportunities of our past; the stone thrown through a window; wasted time; and words already spoken. With this in mind, we must think before we speak!

~Hey, I'm just a "sista" tryin' to tell somebody about JESUS.~

7) Thou shalt not commit adultery (verse 14). The following is written concerning married couples:

> Let the husband render unto the wife due benevolence: and likewise also the wife unto the husband. The wife hath not power of her own body, but the husband: and likewise also the husband hath not power of his own body, but the wife. Defraud ye not one the other, except it be with consent for a time, that ye may give yourselves to fasting and prayer; and come together again, that Satan tempt you not for your incontinency (lacking in moderation or self-control, especially of sexual desire). (1 Corinthians 7:3-5)

A man and woman who are married to one another cannot ration what is due each other. When an individual withholds from his or her spouse out of anger, he or she is opening a door for Satan to get busy in his or her relationship. We are to let nothing or no one come between us and our spouses. "Therefore shall a man leave his father and his mother, and shall cleave unto his wife: and they shall be one flesh" (Genesis 2:24); "For this cause shall a man leave his father and mother, and cleave to his wife; And they twain (two) shall be one flesh: so then they are no more twain (two), but one flesh. What therefore God hath joined together, let not man put asunder" (Mark 10:7-9).

~Hey, I'm just a "sista" tryin' to tell somebody about JESUS.~

It seems that in today's society, sex (sexual intercourse) is the basis for everything. I hear many people say that they will not buy a pair of shoes without trying them on first, and I have heard some say, "Why buy the cow when you can get the milk for free?" (meaning,

"Why should I marry this person when he/she is willing to have sex without this commitment?). Well, to the latter question, this is what the Word says: "For this is the will of God, even your sanctification, that ye should abstain from fornication" (1 Thessalonians 4:3); and in 1 Peter 2:11: "Dearly beloved, I beseech you as strangers and pilgrims, abstain from fleshly lusts, which war against the soul."

Also in response to the latter query, Paul wrote the following:

> Now concerning the things whereof ye wrote unto me: It is *good* for a man *not to* touch a woman. Nevertheless, *to avoid* fornication, let every man have *his own wife*, and let every woman have *her own husband*. ... I say therefore to the unmarried and widows, It is good for them if they abide even as I. But if they cannot contain, *let them marry*: for it is better to marry than to burn. (1 Corinthians 7:1-2, 8-9)

Now this is what is called "soul food." Ladies and gentlemen, believers must *first* establish a relationship with Jesus, accepting Him as our Lord and Savior, and then read and study about Him and what it is that He has in store for us. Believers must learn to appreciate abstinence.

In the beginning, sexual intercourse was designed for the purpose of populating the world. God told Adam the following in the Garden of Eden: "So God created man in his own image, in the image of God created he him; male and female created he them. And God blessed them, and God said unto them, Be fruitful, and multiply, and replenish the earth, and subdue it: and have dominion over the fish of the sea, and over the fowl of the air, and over every living thing that moveth upon the earth" (Genesis 1:27-28).

When sexual intercourse takes place in a relationship—whether it is experienced in the confines of marriage or out of wedlock—it involves intimacy. It is meant to be a consummation of the marriage vows. It involves emotions. It can make or break a relationship. An individual who cannot say beforehand that he or she wants to be with the person with whom he or she is about to "entangle" for the rest of his or her life does not need to get involved sexually with that person. Society asserts that every person with whom one is sexually active is then practically involved (by association) with everyone else who has been involved with that individual. In other words, a person becomes a part of the concubine that Jody has been with, and the same with every man that Rahab has been with. Hence, when we allow our flesh to rule us instead of our ruling our flesh, we subject ourselves to mass destruction.

Virginity on the parts of both male and female is no longer taught (for whatever the reason)—but it is what is best. A couple's maintaining their virginity until marriage allows them to *only have firsthand knowledge of* each other. A person who goes out tasting and sampling—conquering whom he/she will—is truly playing with fire and *will* get burned…especially with sexually transmitted diseases (STDs) like HIV/AIDS, syphilis, gonorrhea, and so forth on the rise; these are things which, if left untreated, can and will kill. "Know ye not that the unrighteous shall not inherit the kingdom of God? Be not deceived: neither fornicators, nor idolaters, nor adulterers, nor effeminate, nor abusers of themselves with mankind, Nor thieves, nor covetous, nor drunkards, nor revilers, nor extortioners, shall inherit the kingdom of God" (1 Corinthians 6:9-10). Clearly, the best way to avoid doom is to avidly try to heed and adhere to the Word of God. Want to go to heaven? It is a destination that is most assuredly real!

~Hey, I'm just a "sista" tryin' to tell somebody about JESUS.~

8) Thou shalt not steal (verse 15). What is stealing? To *steal* is to take the property of another without permission or right—to commit or practice theft. Remember how when we were on our jobs (perhaps, before we got "saved"), and those who were secretaries may have needed office supplies for their home offices; or maybe those who were nurses needed supplies for their first-aid kits; or those janitors among us needed cleaning supplies for their own homes? No matter the logic or justification behind the action, this is S-T-E-A-L-I-N-G! People sometimes reason that certain items are taken as "perks" because they were not getting paid enough on their jobs. "RIGHT!" Regardless of the circumstances, "You didn't buy it, so don't be tryin' it." On the flip side, a person who gets caught taking that which is not his or hers and consequently loses his or her job all of a sudden utters how "It ain't fair!"

Then there is stealing from family members. "I found this twenty-dollar bill in brother's pocket when I did the laundry." Well, evidently it belonged to someone else, so it should not be considered as pay for washing the person's clothes—and neither should the money on "Mama's dresser in her jewelry box" be touched. Ugh! And what about one's signing checks and/or using the ATM card for his or her own purposes and not for the purpose intended—to help his or her senior parents, aunts, and/or uncles? Well, let us get to the main point: "Will a man rob God? Yet ye have robbed me. But ye say, Wherein have we robbed thee? In tithes and offerings" (Malachi 3:8). Okay, so now I am dipping is somebody's business (more to come in chapter 8). We cannot do what Jesus did on the Cross for our sins. Thou shalt not steal! (And we really don't want to be stealing from God!)

~Hey, I'm just a "sista" tryin' to tell somebody about JESUS.~

9) Thou shalt not bear false witness against thy neighbor (verse 16). What does it mean to "bear false witness"? *Bear*: "to transmit or spread: to bear gossip; to render or supply (especially in the phrase, "bear witness"); *false*: "uttering or declaring what is untrue"; *witness*: "a person who gives testimony, as in a court of law; a person who has seen or can give firsthand evidence of some event." So if the word *bear* means "to **spread**," and the word *false* means "**untrue**," and the word *witness* means "to give firsthand **evidence**," then the act of *bearing false witness* is merely lying—and most of the time gossiping. According to 1 Peter 4:15, "Let none of you suffer as a murderer, or as a thief, or as an evildoer, or as a busybody in other men's matters" (KJV); "If you suffer, however, it must not be for murder, stealing, making trouble, or prying into other people's affairs" (NLT [*New Living Translation*]). Oh my goooood-ness!

Is there any more that needs to be said about one's bearing false witness against his or her neighbor? Oh, yes, there is. Who are our neighbors? Our neighbors are members of our race of people. Sounds prejudiced or biased, does it not? Not so…for there is but one race of people—the *human* race: "And the LORD God formed man of the dust of the ground, and breathed into his nostrils the breath of life; and man became a living soul" (Genesis 2:7); "And Adam called his wife's name Eve; because she was the mother of all living" (Genesis 3:20). From Adam and Eve came all of mankind… the human race. There are different cultural backgrounds but only one race—so **all** *are our neighbors*.

We are to teach truth, know truth, and live truth.

10) Thou shalt not covet thy neighbour's house, thou shalt not covet thy neighbour's wife, nor his manservant, nor his maidservant, nor his ox, nor his ass, nor any thing that is thy neighbour's (verse 17). *Covet*: "to desire wrongfully, inordinately, or without due regard for the rights of others: to have an inordinate or wrongful desire (inordinate/unrestrained, as in behavior or emotion)." No one can have his or her neighbor's wife (or husband), or the person's belongings. Each of us is to get our own "Boo" and our own "stuff." Wishing for something that someone else has is coveting—that necklace, that guy, that girl, that car, that bank account, etc. Instead of breaking this commandment, we are to seek after God: "But seek ye first the kingdom of God, and his righteousness; and all these things shall be added unto you" (Matthew 6:33). Halle-luuuuuu-jah any-how!

The ten aforementioned instructions are real. They were not just meant to add entertainment value to a movie or to something to be read; no, there are to be lived. Heaven and hell are very real places—so if we have any doubt about it, wouldn't it be better to live as though heaven and hell are real and then die and find out that they were not, than to live as though they are not real and die and find out that they were real? Think on those things!

God has chosen us to be His people, as outlined in the following Scripture:

But ye are a chosen generation, a royal priesthood, an holy nation, a peculiar people; that ye should shew forth the praises of him who hath called you out of darkness into his marvellous light: Which in time past were not a people, but are now the people of God: which had not obtained mercy, but now have obtained mercy. Dearly beloved, I beseech you as strangers and pilgrims, abstain from fleshly lusts, which war against the soul. (1 Peter 2:9-11)

We would do well to remember that the choices that we make dictate the kind of lives that we live, and that those decisions affect not only us but also everyone involved in our lives. We must pray that we will *abstain from fleshly lusts, which war against the soul.*

~Hey, I'm just a "sista" tryin' to tell somebody about JESUS.~

Chapter 4

JESUS

Now the birth of Jesus Christ was on this wise: When as his mother Mary was espoused to Joseph, before they came together, she was found with child of the Holy Ghost. Then Joseph her husband, being a just man, and not willing to make her a publick example, was minded to put her away privily. But while he thought on these things, behold, the angel of the Lord appeared unto him in a dream, saying, Joseph, thou son of David, fear not to take unto thee Mary thy wife: for that which is conceived in her is of the Holy Ghost. And she shall bring forth a son, and thou shalt call his name JESUS: for he shall save his people from their sins. *Now all this was done, that it might be fulfilled which was spoken of the Lord by the prophet, saying, Behold, a virgin shall be with child, and shall bring forth a son, and they shall call his name Emmanuel, which being interpreted is, God with us. Then Joseph being raised from sleep did as the angel of the Lord had bidden him, and took unto him his wife: And knew her not till she had brought forth her firstborn son: and he called his name JESUS.*—Matthew 1:18-25

    In order to proceed in this writing, it is important to know who JESUS is—for how can one understand the Word of God without knowledge of Him?

    I have heard the song lyrics, "What do you know about Jesus, He's alright!" Yes, He is! I hear preachers say, "He came down through forty-two (and there were, I counted them) burning generations," and I wonder, *what does that mean—forty-two burning generations*? They were burning generations because they did not have the Savior Jesus Christ, and were on their way to the fires of hell. They only knew about His coming. Those forty-two burning generations—from Abraham to David, from David until the carrying away into Babylon, and from the carrying away into Babylon unto Christ—were doomed to the fires of hell because the Savior had not come (see Matthew 1:1-17). They (the preachers) say that He stopped off in Bethlehem of Judea, as we say, on a "cold December morning"—the day we call Christmas. He was born to a virgin named Mary, who was told, "Fear not, Mary: for thou hast found favour with God. And, behold, thou shalt conceive in thy womb, and bring forth a son, and shalt call his name JESUS" (Luke 1:30-31). He came to save the world.

Jesus was born; He grew; He went about doing His Father's business of giving sight to the blind, making the lame to walk, making the dumb to talk, and raising the dead. He fed five thousand-plus people with two fish and five loaves of bread. What a mathematician: number ONE in addition and multiplication. He is excellent in subtraction and division—taking away the sins of this world and placing them upon His shoulders, and separating the wheat from the tares. Then one day He decided to die just to save me…He decided to die just to save everyone!

Jesus knew that sin had crept in and taken a toll on God's children. Jesus is our brother, as evidenced by this verse: "But as many as received him (Jesus), to them gave he power to become the sons of God, even to them that believe on his name" (John 1:12). He was given to the world: "For God so loved the world, that he gave his only begotten Son (Jesus), that whosoever believeth in him should not perish, but have everlasting life. For God sent not his Son into the world to condemn the world; but that the world through him might be saved" (John 3:16-17). He was condemned for our sins—the sins of the whole world. He was sentenced to death by crucifixion (see Luke 23:20-24). He was taken to a place called Calvary (see Luke 23:33).

It was said that Jesus was hung on a cross. It was a cursed, painful, and shameful death—a death accursed by the law *(Cursed is he that hangeth on a tree)*; full of pain, the body was nailed through the nervous parts (the hands and feet), and upon the cross hung all of His weight; His was the demise that was typical with the death of a malefactor or a slave, not of a free man. Jesus was exposed as a public spectacle.

It is written in the Scriptures that Joseph of Arimathea begged for Jesus' body and put Him in his (Joseph's) new tomb (no man had ever laid there, so it was new). Man has said that it was a borrowed tomb because He only needed it for a little while: three days and three nights. I do not know if it was thirty-six hours or seventy-two hours—for Jesus did the math; Jesus said, "For as Jonas was three days and three nights in the whale's belly; so shall the Son of man be three days and three nights in the heart of the earth" (Matthew 12:40); "Jesus answered and said unto them, Destroy this temple, and in three days I will raise it up" (John 2:19). He was talking about raising Himself...after all, He is God: "I and my Father are one" (John 10:30). Check that math here! We see that one plus one equals two; Jesus said, "I and MY Father are one."

(Concerning God's math, we are told this about the Lord's timing: "Beloved, be not ignorant of this one thing, that one day is with the Lord as a thousand years, and a thousand years as one day" (2 Peter 3:8). Check that math! God's ways are not ours to figure out; it is important that we just believe Him.) So back to Jesus' situation: "And very early in the morning the first day of the week, they came unto the sepulchre at the rising of the sun" (Mark 16:2). As the preachers say, "He got up on that third-day morning, the first day of the week, before the rising of the sun...with all power, all power, in heaven and in Earth in His hands. Hallelujah! Hallelujah! Hallelujah! "And many other signs truly did Jesus in the presence of his disciples, which are not written in this book: But these are written, that ye might believe that Jesus is the Christ, the Son of God; and that believing ye might have life through his name" (John 20:30-31).

Jesus died over two thousand years ago. Yet, nobody has ever referred to Him as the *late* Jesus—not even those who do not believe. Nowhere in history has this been the case! Nowhere has He EVER been referred to in the past tense! Why? Because He is the living God!

JESUS: "That at the name of Jesus every knee should bow, of things in heaven, and things in earth, and things under the earth; And that every tongue should confess that Jesus Christ is Lord, to the glory of God the Father" (Philippians 2:10-11). JESUS: "Neither is there salvation in any other: for there is none other name under heaven given among men, whereby we must be saved" (Acts 4:12). JESUS: There was none like Him, nor is there another to come after Him—for He lived a perfect life so that believers may have a chance to receive salvation. In the Hebrew and Greek languages, the words that are used for "salvation" convey the ideas of deliverance, safety, preservation, healing, and soundness. Receiving salvation means being saved from the penalties of sin; so those who have not accepted or will not accept Jesus Christ, the Son of God, to be their Lord and Savior are bound for the penalties of sin.

Paul, the writer of the book of Romans, wrote, "For I am not ashamed of the gospel of Christ; for it is the power of God unto salvation to every one that believeth; to the Jew first, and also to the Greek" (Romans 1:16). (As a paraphrase from writings in *The Scofield Study Bible*, "Salvation for the believer is in the past, present and the future tenses; 1) *he has been* saved, 2) he is *being* saved (ongoing), and 3) he *will be* saved in 'the sense of entire conformity to Christ.'" Salvation comes only by grace through faith in God and belief in His Son, it is a free gift of God and only if we want it can we receive it. It cannot be bought nor can you work for it.) (Refer to Romans 1:16.)

Because of salvation, we work toward the cause of Christ, winning others to join His family of believers; receiving salvation comes about "Not of works, lest any man should boast" (Ephesians 2:9). The following is also said about the way in which believers receive salvation:

> Not by works of righteousness which we have done, but according to his mercy he saved us, by the washing of regeneration, and renewing of the Holy Ghost; Which he shed on us abundantly through Jesus Christ our Saviour; That being justified by his grace, we should be made heirs according to the hope of eternal life. This is a faithful saying, and these things I will that thou affirm constantly, that they which have believed in God might be careful

to maintain good works. These things are good and profitable unto men. (Titus 3:5-8)

Because we have accepted Christ, we strive to turn from the things we did in the past—living in the flesh—things that are not of God: "Therefore if any man be in Christ, he is a new creature: old things are passed away; behold, all things are become new" (2 Corinthians 5:17). As we worship God, we become spiritually minded and conform to the things that are spiritual. We turn away from the following things that are of the flesh:

> Now the works of the flesh are manifest, which are these; Adultery, fornication, uncleanness, lasciviousness, Idolatry, witchcraft, hatred, variance, emulations, wrath, strife, seditions, heresies, Envyings, murders, drunkenness, revellings, and such like: of the which I tell you before, as I have also told you in time past, that they which do such things shall not inherit the kingdom of God. (Galatians 5:19-21)

When we give ourselves over to the power of the Holy Spirit, *we become as new*, striving to demonstrate "the fruit of the Spirit," which is "love, joy, peace, longsuffering, gentleness, goodness, faith, Meekness, temperance: against such there is no law" (Galatians 5:22-23).

~Hey, I'm just a "sista" tryin' to tell somebody about JESUS.~

Chapter 5

Faith

Now faith is the substance of things hoped for, the evidence of things not seen.—Hebrews 11:1

What is faith? From the dictionary point of view, it means having a belief that is not based on proof: it is having confidence in a person or thing; it is belief in God or in the doctrines or teachings of religion. From the Bible, "Now faith is the substance of things hoped for, the evidence of things not seen" (Hebrews 11:1).

How does one obtain faith? "So then *faith* cometh by hearing, and hearing by the word of God" (Romans 10:17). We obtain faith by *hearing the Word of God.* Our belief in God comes from reading and studying His Word, which is our "soul food"—and not the food typically labeled by the black/American-African culture; no, it is the food for our souls, that part of us which will reign with Jesus in heaven *if* we have made the decision to accept Him as our Lord and Savior. Our having faith is a requirement of our receiving salvation through Christ: "Without faith it is impossible to please him: for he that cometh to God must believe that he is, and that he is a rewarder of them that diligently seek him" (Hebrews 11:6). We first have to believe that God is—then we learn to have faith in Him through His Word. And if we do not believe that He is, then HOW can we have any faith in Him?

The following question was presented to a group of people: "Isn't faith and positive thinking the same thing?" No, not necessarily. Positive thinking is said to be a mind-training technique that requires effort on the participant's part in order for him or her to focus on optimistic thoughts (expecting the best outcome), and to remove all negative thoughts. It is said that engaging in positive thinking means one's thinking good or affirmative thoughts, over and over, in order to rid himself or herself of depressing, unhealthy, and negative thoughts. Positive thinking is supposed to help the mind reverse the damaging effects of negative thinking.

This is all well and good; however, having to adhere *strictly* to engaging in positive thinking seems to be a notion of man—whereas having faith is of God. When we think of faith, we are thinking of God. It is not wrong to think positively or to strive to think positively. However, if a person has not confessed with his or her mouth or does not believe in his or her heart that God raised Jesus from the dead, then the person does not have faith and, thus, will not experience eternal life in Christ (see Romans 10:9). Many who trust in the "power of positive thinking" to yield the desired outcomes are trusting in themselves instead of having faith that God will work everything out to the good. Perhaps true "positive thinking" stems from having faith in God.

Faith. It does not take much to have faith. Jesus said that one's having faith as a grain of mustard seed will yield big results—remembering that said faith is in GOD, not in man or in self. We can each ask ourselves this: "Do I have any mountains in my life that need to be removed?" If so, then here is some insight: "And Jesus said unto them, Because of your unbelief: for verily I say unto you, If ye have faith as a grain of mustard seed, ye shall say unto this mountain, Remove hence to yonder place; and it shall remove; and nothing shall be impossible unto you" (Matthew 17:20). A mustard seed is said to be one of the smallest seeds there are, yet it can grow into a great tree—symbolizing that with just a little faith, we can expect great things to happen: "The kingdom of heaven is like to a grain of mustard seed, which a man took, and sowed in his field: Which indeed is the least of all seeds: but when it is grown, it is the greatest among herbs, and becometh a tree, so that the birds of the air come and lodge in the branches thereof" (Matthew 13:31-32).

Faith. People who have faith must take action. An individual can have faith that God will allow his or her car to start, but until he or she puts the key into the ignition and starts it, nothing will happen. James 2:26 reads, "For as the body without the spirit is dead, *so faith without works is dead* also"; "Just as the body is dead without breath, so also faith is dead without good works" (NLT). We can be ever so full of faith, but if we do not take some kind of action, then whatever we want to happen will not work.

How do we know that we have faith? When we are going through a trial or test, the fruit of the Spirit comes forth in us. We are using that faith to believe that God will see us through whatever it is that we are going through. We learn to trust God in all things. We show love, we have joy, and we have peace; "And the peace of God, which passeth all understanding, shall keep your hearts and minds through Christ Jesus" (Philippians 4:7). "Thou wilt keep him in perfect peace, whose mind is stayed on thee: because he trusteth in thee" (Isaiah 26:3). When we have faith, we are patient in our waiting and we can encourage others as we go through. Our faith in God is renewed because we have learned to believe in His Word. "Above all, taking the shield of faith, wherewith ye shall be able to quench all the fiery darts of the wicked" (Ephesians 6:16). The shield of faith is a part of our "spiritual war clothing" that we wear in order to fight off the murmurings of Satan.

The eleventh chapter of the book of Hebrews makes reference to many occasions of faith, from Abel to the prophets. Rahab, a harlot, had heard about "the God of Israel" when she hid the spies. She had enough faith in their God, because her actions could have cost her her life and the lives of her family members. (Her story can be found in the book of Joshua, chapter 2; read her story.)

"Now the just shall live by faith: but if any man draw back, my soul shall have no pleasure in him" (Hebrews 10:38). Romans 1:17 reads, "For therein is the righteousness of God revealed from faith to faith: as it is written, The just shall live by faith"; "This Good News tells us how God makes us right in his sight. This is accomplished from start to finish by faith. As the Scriptures say, 'It is through faith that a righteous person has life'" (NLT).

Isn't it better to have life? Trust God. Have faith in Him. Live.

~Hey, I'm just a "sista" tryin' to tell somebody about JESUS.~

Chapter 6

Teachers—Teaching Prayer

And when thou prayest, thou shalt not be as the hypocrites are: for they love to pray standing in the synagogues and in the corners of the streets, that they may be seen of men. Verily I say unto you, They have their reward. But thou, when thou prayest, enter into thy closet, and when thou hast shut thy door, pray to thy Father which is in secret; and thy Father which seeth in secret shall reward thee openly. But when ye pray, use not vain repetitions, as the heathen do: for they think that they shall be heard for their much speaking. Be not ye therefore like unto them: for your Father knoweth what things ye have need of, before ye ask him. After this manner therefore pray ye: Our Father which art in heaven, Hallowed be thy name. Thy kingdom come, Thy will be done in earth, as it is in heaven. Give us this day our daily bread. And forgive us our debts, as we forgive our debtors. And lead us not into temptation, but deliver us from evil: For thine is the kingdom, and the power, and the glory, for ever. Amen. For if ye forgive men their trespasses, your heavenly Father will also forgive you: But if ye forgive not men their trespasses, neither will your Father forgive your trespasses.—Matthew 6:5-15

What is prayer? According to the dictionary, *prayer* is "a personal communication or petition addressed to a deity (God), especially in the form of supplication (humbly asking), adoration, praise, contrition (sincere penitence or regret) or thanksgiving." It is also a term used to describe any other form of spiritual communion with a deity. It is the form of communication that is required to commune with God, our heavenly Father.

Why pray? We pray because we are instructed to do so: "And he spake a parable unto them to this end, that men ought always to pray, and not to faint" (Luke 18:1); "Pray without ceasing" (1 Thessalonians 5:17). It is our duty to pray, and we should commit to doing it regularly.

Where and when do we pray? We can pray on our jobs, in school, in our homes with family, during personal prayer times, in our "secret closets," and so forth. Actually, whenever and wherever the opportunity presents itself, we should take time to pray. Now, while on the job and at school—the places where we have obligations to meet with others to fulfill certain tasks—we should engage in prayer on our time only…like during lunch and break times, not during company time. H-E-L-L-OOOOO!

Praying is our way of asking God to keep us from sin, to supply what it is that we need—praying for each other, praying for a better understanding of His Word, and praying to hear from Him. When we pray, we should *listen* in order to hear what He has to say to us. Matthew 6:5-15 comprises what some call "The Lord's Prayer"—but, actually, The Lord's Prayer is the entire seventeenth chapter of the book of John. The Model Prayer is found in Matthew 6:5-15. It was what Jesus taught His disciples when they asked of Him to teach them to pray (see Luke 11:1). Let's take a moment to review Matthew 6:5-15 (provided at the very beginning of this chapter).

In Matthew 6:5-15, Jesus addressed His disciples on how to pray as well as how *not* to pray. He addressed how the hypocrites prayed, wanting to be seen of men to appear more holy than they actually were, and they wanted to be praised because they "said a lot." Ever heard the phrase, "less is more"? I think this might have been on the order that Jesus was speaking about. One can speak many words in a prayer, but if his or her heart is not right before God, then it is all in vain. In verses 6 and 7 of Matthew 6, reference is made to where to go to pray, and to not use vain repetitions (saying the same thing over and over)—remembering that Jesus considers what is in our hearts, while man looks at our outward appearance. Sometimes we get caught up in praying and think that the more we say the better we sound, not even thinking about what God is saying of us. We must remember that our prayers are our communication with Him. Thank God for His Holy Spirit. "Likewise the Spirit also helpeth our infirmities: *for we know not what we should pray for* as we ought:

but the Spirit itself maketh intercession for us with groanings which cannot be uttered. And he that searcheth the hearts knoweth what is the mind of the Spirit, because he maketh intercession for the saints according to the will of God" (Romans 8:26-27).

How do we pray? The Model Prayer starts off by giving recognition to God—who He is, where He is, and His character. ***Our Father which art in heaven, Hallowed be thy name***: Who is He? He is God our heavenly Father; we acknowledge that He is our Father—after all, He did create us. We are giving reverence to Him and to His position…and to the fact that He is Father to all; He is not just *mine*: He is *ours*. Where is He? Our Father is the one who ***art in heaven***—the place where He resides—yet He is everywhere… *omnipresent*. What is His character like? He is regarded as holy and sacred. There is none like Him and He alone is God, as is relayed in Mark 12:32—"And the scribe said unto him, Well, Master, thou hast said the truth: for there is one God; and there is none other but he"; and in Ephesians 4:6—"One God and Father of all, who is above all, and through all, and in you all." Once we realize *who* God is, realizing that "For *in him we live, and move, and have our being*" (Acts 17:28a), we can then come into a better relationship with Him—we can pray to Him with the knowledge that He is to be reverenced as holy and sacred, He is omnipresent…He is *ours*.

Thy kingdom come, Thy will be done in earth, as it is in heaven. In continuing to address the concept of *how we pray*, we are to do so in submission to His greatness and (with respect to His power) His omnipotence. We must recognize that He is in control of the universe, which is comprised of the heavens, the Earth, the waters (and everything that is contained in the waters), humankind, and animal and plant life. Whether we know it or not, whether we like it or not, God is in control of every existential detail that we could ever fathom.

Give us this day our daily bread. We are to pray with the knowledge that God will supply our every need: "But my God shall supply all your need according to his riches in glory by Christ Jesus" (Philippians 4:19). We are to ask for not just what we want, but what we need as well. It is just a matter of not taking Him for granted—as though He just *has* to do it for us. He does, however, willingly provide for us…because He loves us so. We are fortunate that Jesus instructs us to ask, and gives us instructions on *how* to ask: *"Ask, and it shall be given you; seek, and ye shall find; knock, and it shall be opened unto you"* (Matthew 7:7); "And whatsoever ye shall ask in my name, that will I do, that the Father may be glorified in the Son" (John 14:13); "If ye abide in me, and my words abide in you, ye shall ask what ye will, and it shall be done unto you" (John 15:7). (In the Bible, the words of the preceding three verses are written in red—representing the words spoken by Jesus Himself.)

And forgive us our debts, as we forgive our debtors. Another aspect of how we are to pray to God (which is probably one of the most important requests in this prayer that all should be made aware of) is that we must ask for forgiveness and we must forgive others in order to be forgiven.

And lead us not into temptation, but deliver us from evil. I was once told by a person of another faith that in praying this prayer, I was praying for my destruction. Of course I asked why that was the case. I was told that in order for God's kingdom to come on Earth as it is in heaven, the evil here had to be destroyed; also, the question was posed of why God would lead us into temptation. Needless to say, I just asked that the Lord have mercy on that person—for "they knew not what they were saying." I think the individual had forgotten about the words of Romans 10:9: "That if thou shalt confess with thy mouth the Lord Jesus, and shalt believe in thine heart that God hath raised him from the dead, thou shalt be saved." We must pray in this manner, first of all, because Jesus said for us to do so—and, second, because when we accept Jesus as Lord and Savior of and over our lives, Satan gets busy: "Be sober, be vigilant; because your adversary the devil, as a roaring lion, walketh about, seeking whom he may devour" (1 Peter 5:8). Remember what happened in chapter 4? Jesus was born to a virgin, which made Him part human…yet still fully divine. Jesus, as a man who experienced what we go through, was tempted of Satan ("Then was Jesus led up of the Spirit into the wilderness to be tempted of the devil" [Matthew 4:1]), *after* He was baptized by John. Just as Christ was tempted, we will be tempted—and the request, "lead us not into temptation," is merely our admitting to our weakness and asking for help in our weakness.

Without God, we can do nothing in and of ourselves. We need His divine intervention, His Word, to keep us from the "snares and tricks" of the devil.

For thine is the kingdom, and the power, and the glory, for ever. Amen. Here, again, when we pray, we are to recognize His omnipresence, His omnipotence, and that all glory belongs to Him forever. Amen…it is so!

There are several instances in the Bible of where prayer went forth from people who adhered to the Matthew 6 way to pray: Abraham prayed; Jacob prayed; Moses prayed for the people; Joshua prayed; Manoah prayed, regarding the birth of his son; Samson prayed for strength against the Philistines; Hannah prayed for a son (Samuel); David prayed; Solomon prayed for wisdom; Hezekiah, when he became deathly ill, prayed and God granted him fifteen years to be added to his life; Daniel prayed; Shadrach, Meshach, and Abednego prayed; Jonah prayed from inside the belly of the fish; and Jesus prayed (see John 17). There is not a better example to follow than Jesus'.

~Hey, I'm just a "sista" tryin' to tell somebody about JESUS.~

Chapter 7

Teachers—Teaching Love

*He that loveth not knoweth not GOD;
for GOD is love.*—1 John 4:8

Often, love is referred to as a strong feeling between two people—a strong feeling that one has for another. It is said that love is an action word, and that love is as love does. In studying the Bible, we are taught to love: "Beloved, let us love one another: for love is of God; and every one that loveth is born of God, and knoweth God" (1 John 4:7).

In conducting my research for this writing, I came across these kinds of love (in the Greek form): *storge*: "parental affection; the instinctive affection which animals have for their young"; *phileo*: "love between family and friends"; *eros*: "romantic love between husband and wife"; and *agape*: "unconditional love." *Agape* love is the love that God has for us and the kind of love that we are to have for each other. God loves us so much that He gave… "For God so loved the world, that he gave his only begotten Son, that whosoever believeth in him should not perish, but have everlasting life" (John 3:16). And this is the action part of love: "Greater love hath no man than this, that a man lay down his life for his friend" (John 15:13).

God loves us unconditionally. There is nothing that can separate us from His love. "For I am persuaded, that neither death, nor life, nor angels, nor principalities, nor powers, nor things present, nor things to come, Nor height, nor depth, nor any other creature, shall be able to separate us from the *love* of God, which is in Christ Jesus our Lord" (Romans 8:38-39). In chapter 1, we noted that Jesus gave us the power to become the sons (and daughters) of God: "But as many as received him, to them gave he power to become the sons of

God, even to them that believe on his name: Which were born, not of blood, nor of the will of the flesh, nor of the will of man, but of God" (John 1:12-13). God loves us (unconditionally) through His Son, Jesus. God gave His Son, Jesus, so that we would not have to face eternal damnation in the fires of hell for our sins. Though God loves us unconditionally, *there is a condition* for our salvation—for our being saved from the fires of hell: *we must* accept His Son, Jesus, believing that He died on a cross (the most humiliating way to die, especially having done nothing wrong), and that God, His Father, raised Him from the dead. There are some who perhaps say, "Now how am I supposed to believe in somebody whom I have not met, have not seen, and (some may even say) have never even heard of?" The following Scripture should help to answer this question:

> That if thou shalt confess with thy mouth the Lord Jesus, and shalt believe in thine heart that God hath raised him from the dead, thou shalt be saved. For with the heart man believeth unto righteousness; and with the mouth confession is made unto salvation. For the scripture saith, Whosoever believeth on him shall not be ashamed. For there is no difference between the Jew and the Greek: for the same Lord over all is rich unto all that call upon him. For whosoever shall call upon the name of the Lord shall be saved. How then shall they call on him in whom they have not believed? and how shall they believe in him of whom they have not heard? and how shall they hear without a preacher? And how shall they preach, except they be sent? as it is written, How beautiful are the feet of them that preach the gospel of peace, and bring glad tidings of good things! (Romans 10:9-15)

There is no excuse for those who have a means through which to hear about Jesus to not know about Jesus. Case in point: *Hey, I'm just a "sista" tryin' to tell somebody about JESUS*—and anyone who has been reading this book now knows something about Him. And those who know about Jesus should be able to teach others about the love of Jesus; this is a command from Jesus Himself: "A new commandment I give unto you, That ye love one another; as I have loved you, that ye also love one another" (John 13:34)—because we are God's children, Jesus' disciples: "By this shall all men know that ye are my disciples, if ye have love one to another" (John 13:35); "And now, Israel, what doth the LORD thy God require of thee, but to fear the LORD thy God, to walk in all his ways, and to love him, and to serve the LORD thy God with all thy heart and with all thy soul, To keep the commandments of the LORD, and his statutes, which I command thee this day for thy good?" (Deuteronomy 10:12-13). All should be able to see love in us as we exhibit Christian character.

~Hey, I'm just a "sista" tryin' to tell somebody about JESUS.~

In loving God, as previously noted, there is a requirement for us to love one another. So many times we say that we love someone, but we do not like him or her. Is there really a difference? To *like* something or someone means "to be suitable or agreeable to; to feel attraction toward or take pleasure in; to feel toward: regard; to feel inclined: choose, prefer." God created all of mankind—having done so in His image and likeness—and since He loves unconditionally, we are to love unconditionally, regardless of who the object of our love is. "Like" and "love" fall into the same category as affection (in this respect). While there may be something that we do not like about an individual, we still have to love him or her. "Thou shalt not avenge, nor bear any grudge against the children of thy people, but thou shalt love thy neighbour as thyself: I am the LORD" (Leviticus 19:18).

We have to understand that God made us in His image and likeness, and "we were good and very good": "So God created man in his own image, in the image of God created he him; male and female created he them. ... And God saw every thing that he had made, and, behold, it was very good. And the evening and the morning were the sixth day" (Genesis 1:27, 31). So with that being said, who are we to say that we do not like someone whom God created? The Pharisees, who were members of the Jewish sect and were known for their strict adherence to the *written* law during the time of Jesus' ministry on Earth, asked Him these questions: "Master, which is the great commandment in the law? Jesus said unto him, Thou shalt love the Lord thy God with all thy heart, and with all thy soul, and with all thy mind. This is the first and great commandment. And the second is like unto it, Thou shalt love thy neighbour as thyself. On these two commandments hang all the law and the prophets" (Matthew 22:36-40). In loving God, we are to keep His commandments; we are to be obedient through His Word—the Holy Scriptures.

Yes, we can choose to be ignorant of the Word of God; however, that term that "ignorance is bliss" is not a true statement when it comes to pleasing God, our heavenly Father. We are held to some level of accountability for everything that we say and do, whether we know better or not; as a reminder of this, refer to the following: "And that servant, which knew his lord's will, and prepared not himself, neither did according to his will, shall be beaten with many stripes. But he that knew not, and did commit things worthy of stripes, shall be beaten with few stripes. For unto whomsoever much is given, of him shall be much required: and to whom men have committed much, of him they will ask the more" (Luke 12:47-48).

In loving God, we are also required to love our enemies. Say what! *That man who just molested me! That woman who slept with my husband! That boy who just took my son's life because he didn't like him—and that little girl who told my daughter that she was stupid and ugly, causing my daughter to commit suicide!* GOD, YOU HAVE GOT TO BE KIDDING! Love my enemies? We can glean much guidance from Scripture regarding this stance: "But I say unto you, Love your enemies, bless them that curse you, do good to them that hate you, and pray for them which despitefully use you, and persecute you" (Matthew 5:44); "Dearly beloved, avenge not yourselves, but rather give place unto wrath: for it is written, Vengeance is mine; I will repay, saith the Lord. Therefore if thine enemy hunger, feed him; if he thirst, give him drink: for in so doing thou shalt heap coals of fire on his head. Be not overcome of evil, but overcome evil with good" (Romans 12:19-21). Our being kind to or loving our enemies is a hard thing to do when we do not have a relationship with God—which is why we must refer to the following verses: "I can do all things through Christ which strengtheneth me"

(Philippians 4:13); "But Jesus beheld them, and said unto them, With men this is impossible; but with God all things are possible" (Matthew 19:26). *No prayer, no power; little prayer, little power; much prayer, much power! Hallelujah!*

In loving God, it is important for us to understand that obedience is better than sacrifice: "And Samuel said, Hath the Lord as great delight in burnt offerings and sacrifices, as in obeying the voice of the Lord? Behold, to obey is better than sacrifice, and to hearken than the fat of rams" (1 Samuel 15:22). During the time of the writing of that verse, animal sacrifices were offered to God for atonement for sin or in worship of God; God was ultimately seeking humanity's obedience to HIM. Our being obedient to God is a sign of our love for Him. When we are deliberately disobedient—when we make the choice to do what the Holy Spirit is telling us *not* to do, or to deliberately *not* do what it is that He has told us to do—there are consequences to be suffered. Realize this: God is in control, whether we like it or not. "Know ye that the Lord he is God: it is he that hath made us, and not we ourselves; we are *his* people, and the sheep of *his* pasture" (Psalm 100:3).

~Hey, I'm just a "sista" tryin' to tell somebody about JESUS.~

Chapter 8

Teachers—Teaching about Giving

*Even from the days of your fathers ye are gone away from mine ordinances, and have not kept them. Return unto me, and I will return unto you, saith the L*ORD *of hosts. But ye said, Wherein shall we return? Will a man rob God? Yet ye have robbed me. But ye say, Wherein have we robbed thee? In tithes and offerings. Ye are cursed with a curse: for ye have robbed me, even this whole nation. Bring ye all the tithes into the storehouse, that there may be meat in mine house, and prove me now herewith, saith the L*ORD *of hosts, if I will not open you the windows of heaven, and pour you out a blessing, that there shall not be room enough to receive it.*—Malachi 3:7-10

  The instruction to give, according to the aforementioned Scripture passage, was a part of God's plan for His people to support His church, the Temple—"that there would be meat in [His] house"; in doing so, blessings would be poured out beyond measure. We should trust God in our giving enough to believe that He will do what He says He will do. We go to a place to worship. It is just like our homes—we have to pay for electricity, gas, water, telephone service, and whatever it takes to support the home; so it is for God's house. Monetary support is needed if a church is to function properly.
  During Levitical times, there were the Levites and the priests. The Levites were the descendants of Aaron and from them, priests were chosen, ordained, and set apart by God for the purpose of the "care and administration of holy things." They were consecrated to God as His "peculiar people." In tithing, what was offered was one-tenth of possessions—i.e., the land (fruit of the field, trees),

and animals (both good and bad, as it is said in research that the animals were counted with the shepherd's staff and whichever tenth one came under his staff was the one given as the tithe). It was a common practice for the people to bring a tithe to the Temple for the Levites (the priests), who performed the religious ceremonies, for their maintenance; and out of this, they (the Levites) were to dedicate a tenth to God to be used by the high priest in performing his duties and for festival purposes. The festival purposes were for the strangers, the fatherless, and the widows (see Deuteronomy 12:5-18). Again, while we should not set out to be obedient and faithful in tithing for the purpose of reaping a reward, there *are* blessings in obedience and faithfulness.

The subject of tithing in the twenty-first century seems to be a very "touchy" one in the church today. Our economy presents the thought, "Well I just don't have that kind of money to give to the church; I can't afford to give 10 percent." However, no one can afford to *not* give 10 percent! Just take a look at what the Lord can do: "Bring ye all the tithes into the storehouse, that there may be meat in mine house, and prove me now herewith, saith the LORD of hosts, if I will not open you the windows of heaven, and pour you out a blessing, that there shall not be room enough to receive it" (Malachi 3:10).

In understanding tithing, it seems that God is telling us that if we trust Him when giving our tenth, then because of our obedience to Him, He will open the windows of heaven and pour out blessings beyond our ability to receive them. In other words, we just cannot imagine the return on such an investment that is fail-proof. There is no stock market crash to suffer. With God's ATM ("A Transcendent Master"), the amount of daily withdrawals is unlimited, there are no transaction fees, and there is truly no identity theft. We can rest assured that God "will rebuke the devourer for [our] sakes, and he shall not destroy the fruits of [our] ground; neither shall [our] vine cast her fruit before the time in the field" (Malachi 3:11). By the same token, if, in our giving, we do not do as God has commanded us to do, then we will notice a reversal of the same Scripture. In teaching tithing, it should be taught that we are to give a tenth of our time, our talents, and our finances. The time is our commitment to

God; our talents (singing, praying, preaching, helping, encouraging, etc.)—whatever God has gifted us with—are to be used to His glory; and our money is to be used for the building up of the church—*"that there may be meat in mine house…saith the* LORD *of hosts."*

Our time. Each of us should ask ourselves, "How much time do I spend with God?" Is it just on Sundays when we go to Sunday school, morning worship service, or afternoon fellowship? Is it when we go to Bible class on the scheduled day of the week at our respective churches? What about prayer? Do we go to prayer meetings to pray as a part of the body of believers? What other activities do we participate in that are God-centered? Do we engage in personal prayer lives and time with God daily? Do we read and study His Word daily in order to be approved by Him? And that time that we *do* spend with Him, is it for a show to the world, or is it done out of the desire to come to know God and what it is that He expects from us as His children?

There are twenty-four hours in a day, and 168 hours in a week. On Sunday, we spend approximately 6.75 hours in church—from Sunday school through afternoon service (if there is any). Mission meetings (if there are any) last approximately one hour. Bible study lasts about 1.5 hours, for a total of 9.25 hours. *Wow! I really spend time with God! I am doing great!*…so we think. Hmm…10 percent of 168 hours is 16.8 hours. We still have 7.55 hours left for God. Well, what's up? For all that He is doing for us right now, in reading this, we should be giving Him more than the tenth. So what is it that has us so bound that we cannot or will not give God any of our time? Just food for thought! What if God did not give us "time"— time to accept Him or to accept His Son, Jesus? Time to breathe, speak, touch, taste, smell, see, hear? What if?

Our talents. What is a *talent*? It is "an innate ability, an aptitude, or an above-average ability; any of various ancient units of weight and money." Talent, used in this context, is with regard to the abilities with which God has endowed us, which should be used to His glory. Everyone should assess the following: What is my talent? Am I a good singer? Is what I do for the glory of God, or do I do what I do to impress "this world"? Do I pray? And when I do, is it for the glory of God—giving thanks to Him—or is it for show, to give the appearance of holiness? When (if) I deliver the Gospel message, is it to win souls to Christ, or for the "Benjamins"? There are many things that can be done for kingdom building. The skills/talents that a person uses to fulfill the requirements of his or her job should be used to help out in his or her church. Romans 12:5-8 (NIV) serves as a breakdown of this sentiment:

> So in Christ we who are many form one body, and each member belongs to all the others. We have different gifts, according to the grace given us. If a man's gift is prophesying, let him use it in proportion to his faith. If it is serving, let him serve; if it is teaching, let him teach; if it is encouraging, let him encourage; if it is contributing to the needs of others, let him give generously; if it is leadership, let him govern diligently; if it is showing mercy, let him do it cheerfully.

There are many ministries in the church, so why should we not be a part of them and give God the glory in all that we do?

Our finances. The church is to be supported by tithes and offerings. The following question was asked once during a meeting: "Can a person work out his tithes by doing something around the church like sweeping the floor or cleaning?" The answer was yes. However, can a person go to the electric company and sweep the floor or do some cleaning with the expectation of keeping his or her lights on? Need anymore be said? We buy designer clothes and accessories. We buy automobiles in some instances that cost sometimes more than the houses we live in. We spend thousands of dollars on technology for ourselves and for our children; but, when it comes to God, we are pinching a dollar.

God has blessed us with life. Jesus has said that He came so that we might have life and have it more abundantly: "The thief cometh not, but for to steal, and to kill, and to destroy: I am come that they might have life, and that they might have it more abundantly" (John 10:10). What does it mean to have something *abundantly*? Having something *abundantly* means having an extremely plentiful or oversufficient quantity. Ten percent of one dollar is one dime. A person can easily give that amount of money and still have ninety cents left to work with. Okay, so there is not much that can be bought with ninety cents anymore—but how about 10 percent of $300,000? That is $30,000. After giving $30,000, one would have $270,000 left to work with. How about that? All God is asking for is the *tenth*; and it is not like He "needs" it…He just wants our obedience to and our faith and trust in Him. We could never repay Him for what He has done, is doing, or will do for us. We are rewarded for our diligence in seeking Him: "But without faith it is impossible to please him: for he that cometh to God must believe that he is, and that he is a rewarder of them that diligently seek him" (Hebrews 11:6); "And prove me now herewith, saith the LORD of hosts, if I will not open you the windows of heaven, and pour you out a blessing, that there shall not be room enough to receive it" (Malachi 3:10b). (Read in Psalm 103 about the rewards that we can look forward to just for our being obedient. No man can offer such.)

  Giving to God is not all of the giving that we are required to do. We need to give to those who are less fortunate than we are: "Pure religion and undefiled before God and the Father is this, To visit the fatherless and widows in their affliction, and to keep himself unspotted from the world" (James 1:27). God is pleased in our giving, as is iterated in the following:

> But this I say, He which soweth sparingly shall reap also sparingly; and he which soweth bountifully shall reap also bountifully. Every man according *as he purposeth in his heart, so let him give; not grudgingly, or of necessity: for God loveth a cheerful giver* (if you are not giving from your heart and willingly, it is best not to give). And God is able to make all grace abound toward you; that ye, always having all sufficiency in all things, may abound to every good work: (As it is written, He hath dispersed abroad; he hath given to the poor: his righteousness remaineth for ever. Now he that ministereth seed to the sower both minister bread for your food, and

multiply your seed sown, *and increase the fruits of your righteousness.* (2 Corinthians 9:6-10)

"I have shewed you all things, how that so labouring ye ought to support the weak, and to remember the words of the Lord Jesus, how he said, It is more blessed to give than to receive" (Acts 20:35). Think about that. For some, the economy is in such turmoil that they are struggling to make ends meet. They are dependent upon others for help and it may be that the church will (if not already the case) become the source of aid for those in need. We must have the desire to give, as well as the desire to be in a *position* to give.

It is so amazing how effectively we function in our places/positions outside of the church: places of employment, hair and nail appointments, dinner reservations, at the movies—all things that tickle our lusts. We are on time every day, no matter what time our workday starts; but on Sunday morning, Sunday school at most churches starts at 9:00 or 9:30 a.m., and our response is "Hey! I get triple time on Sundays; it's the weekend…that's too early, and it's my only day to sleep in." Hmm…just suppose it was a permanent sleep? For just one week, 16.8 hours is not a lot of time to spend on God. There are twenty-four hours in a day, so what problem is there to give two hours and forty minutes of the day to God? We can give Him time during that workday on that j-o-b that He gave us just by saying, "Thank You, Lord, for this job, for this day, for this moment." We ask for so much from Him that He may or may not fulfill (because He knows what is best for us), yet we never stop to say, "Thank You, Lord." While we should give God more than a tenth of what He has blessed us with, that is all He asks of us—one-tenth. We must determine whether we will give to Him of our time, our talents, and our means. Think about it!

~Hey, I'm just a "sista" tryin' to tell somebody about JESUS.~

Chapter 9

Teachers: Men and Women

But speak thou the things which become sound doctrine: That the aged men be sober, grave, temperate, sound in faith, in charity, in patience. The aged women likewise, that they be in behaviour as becometh holiness, not false accusers, not given to much wine, teachers of good things; That they may teach the young women to be sober, to love their own husbands, to love their children, To be discrete, chaste, keepers at home, good, obedient to their own husbands, that the word of God be not blasphemed. Young men likewise exhort to be sober minded. In all things shewing thyself a pattern of good works: in doctrine shewing uncorruptness, gravity, sincerity, Sound speech, that cannot be condemned; that he that is of the contrary part may be ashamed, having no evil thing to say of you.—Titus 2:1-8

To paraphrase, we are to speak that which is suitable and appropriate, that which comes from a sound mind—using good judgment and wisdom, and holding on to our faith and trust in God through adhering to His Word. Though verse 2 refers to the "aged men" who are to be sober, *grave, temperate,* and *sound in faith, in charity, and in patience*, it also applies to women as well, as it is written in that Scripture: "the aged women *likewise*"—with the word *likewise* meaning "in the same manner," "also," and, "in addition to." We are to be the same: *sober* (quiet and calm in our demeanors); *grave* (serious and solemn); *temperate* (moderate and self-restrained); *sound in faith* (grounded, steadfast, and unwavering in our faith in God); *in charity* (meaning, "*to love*"); and *in patience* (quiet, steady, persevering, and even-tempered). These are the characteristics of them who are of the faith: Christians—men and women of God.

The aged men and women. What does it mean to be "aged"? The word *aged* means "brought to maturity or mellowness, such as wine, cheese, or wood: then, older/mature: a period of human life, measured by years from birth, usually marked by a certain stage or degree of mental or physical development and involving legal responsibility and capacity." The aged—older/mature men and women—must behave in ways that lead to their living lives of holiness. It is written: "Sanctify yourselves therefore, and be ye holy: for I am the LORD your God. ... And ye shall be holy unto me: for I the LORD am holy, and have severed you from other people, that ye should be mine" (Leviticus 20:7, 26). We should demonstrate Christian character wherever we go; we should be Christ-like at all times. This is a command from God. There are some Christians (or, as some say, "churchgoers") who may not yet have a relationship with God so they think that they do not have to quite follow God's Word. Some may say, "That is from the Old Testament, and the church came about in the New Testament." Well, to that, here is some New Testament: "Because it is written, Be ye holy; for I am holy" (1 Peter 1:16). Let it be known that the Old and New Testaments support each other.

We have to heed the whole Bible. It is not the Old Country Buffet, where one can get a little of this or a little of that—nor is it Burger King, where one can "have it [his/her] way." Second Timothy 3:16 provides words on this sentiment: "All scripture is given by inspiration of God, and is profitable for doctrine, for reproof, for correction, for instruction in righteousness." And concerning the thought that one's not quite having a relationship with God yet does not mean that he or she is exempt from following His Word, let us reiterate Luke 12:47-48: "And that servant, which knew his lord's will, and prepared not himself, neither did according to his will, shall be beaten with many stripes. But he that knew not, and did commit things worthy of stripes, shall be beaten with few stripes. For unto whomsoever much is given, of him shall be much required: and to whom men have committed much, of him they will ask the more." Here is the same Scripture from another translation: "And a servant who knows what the master wants, but isn't prepared and doesn't carry out those instructions, will be severely punished. But someone who does not know, and then does something wrong, will be punished only lightly. When someone has been given much, much will be required in return; and when someone has been entrusted with much, even more will be required" (NLT). Those of us who are parents should think about when we discipline our children when they are in the first learning stages…it is the same with God: we are His children and we are learning every day.

Our Christian character is very important in our walks with God and in our witnessing to others. It has been said that as Christian men and women, we may be the only Bible that another will see in order to be won to Christ. If we are not living the type of life that God requires us to live, then we cannot be effective witnesses; the seeds that we think we are planting will fall on stony ground and will not take root. "Some fell upon stony places, where they had not much earth: and forthwith they sprung up, because they had no deepness of earth: And when the sun was up, they were scorched; and because they had no root, they withered away" (Matthew 13:5-6). It is often said that actions speak louder than words. How true. If I am telling somebody that the body is the temple of God, and that he or she should not be drinking and getting drunk, yet I am holding a "40 ounce" and the person is having to hold me up, what kind of message am I sending to that person?

The words of Dorothy Law Nolte, in her writing entitled, *Children Learn What They Live: Parenting to Inspire Values* (co-authored by Rachel Harris), are very true. Just as children learn from what they live—from what they see and hear—adults learn in the same way. We influence and are influenced in the same manner, and if we are not strong in the Word of God, we could be sending the wrong message and leading someone wrong (or be led wrong ourselves). As we walk with God, our walks must be in alignment with the Holy Spirit, with His Holy Scriptures. As we teach others—men, women, boys, and girls—we must be sure that our walk matches our talk. How can we tell somebody about Jesus yet not know Him or know about Him ourselves? Our walk and our talk must line up. When our vehicles of transportation yield an uneven, off-balance ride, where the steering veers to the right or left, this is usually an indication that it is time for a front-end alignment. And so it is with our walks with the Lord: we need a "spiritual alignment." We must be in line with the Holy Spirit. "Can two walk together, except they be agreed?" (Amos 3:3).

When two people try to walk together, with one person starting his or her stride on the left foot and the other starting on the right foot, see how off-balance the pair becomes. It is the same with God. He is always right—so we need to be in line with Him. We have to be prayed up and studying His Word when we are trying to tell somebody about Jesus: "Study to shew thyself approved unto God, a workman that needeth not to be ashamed, rightly dividing the word of truth" (2 Timothy 2:15); here are the words of Titus 1:16 (from both the KJV and NLT, respectively): "They profess that they know God; but in works they deny him, being abominable, and disobedient, and unto every good work reprobate"; "Such people claim they know God, but they deny him by the way they live. They are detestable and disobedient, worthless for doing anything good." Wow! I would not want to be in that category.

Let's remember that we lead by example and we lead by following the Word of God, trusting in His Word to lead us in the way that we should go and in helping us to be the effective witnesses that He has called us to be (as in the Great Commission of Matthew 28:18-20).

Let's remember that as we are watching others in their walks—whether they are in Christ or not—we, too, are being watched. For instance, there are some of us who have probably been on their jobs when someone witnessed them doing something that "the person" thinks that they should not be doing…and the first thing out of that person's mouth is, "And you call yourself a Christian!" It is a good statement because it makes one stop and think about what the issue is with that individual; and utterance of that statement is an opportunity to witness to that individual in order to let him or her know (especially if what he or she was witnessing was something that he or she wanted to see because it was out of character for them) that God does not operate in the negative in order to please a nonbeliever. I remember an instance years ago when I was on my job; I had set up my workspace and observed a co-worker removing some items for his use. I stopped him and those were his exact words: "And you call yourself a Christian." My response was, "If you know the actions of a Christian, then you should be one and prepare your workspace as well." I actually won that young man over with that statement. He thought about what he was saying and apologized for challenging me. I was able to plant a seed. Whether or not he accepted the Lord I do not know; but his disposition changed tremendously and we became *true* co-workers.

God does not want us to offend; but, I do not think that He wants us to be offended, either—as is evidenced in Romans 12:20: "Therefore if thine enemy hunger, feed him; if he thirst, give him drink: for in so doing thou shalt heap coals of fire on his head."

~Hey, I'm just a "sista" tryin' to tell somebody about JESUS.~

Chapter 10

Teachers—Teaching Behavior

(As Becometh Holiness...Uncorruptness...Sound Speech [Titus 2:3, 7-8])

But the LORD said unto Samuel, Look not on his countenance, or on the height of his stature; because I have refused him: for the LORD seeth not as man seeth; for man looketh on the outward appearance, but the LORD looketh on the heart.—1 Samuel 16:7

Sisters... A part of our Christian character is informed by our appearance.

In the Scripture above, the reference is to the heart of humanity before God. God sees us through His Son, Jesus. He is looking at our state of being in reference to being His children. As a holy people, we need to strive for holiness with our speech, our actions, and our attire: "In like manner also, that women adorn themselves in *modest apparel*, with shamefacedness and sobriety; not with broided hair, or gold, or pearls, or costly array; But (which becometh women professing godliness) with good works" (1 Timothy 2:9-10).

How many times have we as ladies tried to have a conversation with gentlemen who are talking *at* us, instead of talking *to* us? Ever wonder why? It is because oftentimes the man is talking at what he sees and not to the woman herself. We do our hair and dress to impress, right? But who or what are we trying to impress? We want to *attract, not distract*. Our Christianity is centered on giving glory to God in all of our thoughts, words, and deeds—it is not centered on us. We want to attract attention in a way that makes another person ponder, "What is it about them that is so attractive? They always have smiles on their faces, they never seem worried about anything, and they are always saying, 'Hallelujah—thank You, Jesus!' What is that about? Who is this 'Jesus'?"

I, as a Christian, once decided to do something different with my hair. It was very different to the extent that someone very close to me asked, "What are you selling; what are you advertising?" I was so embarrassed that I hurried to make another change—and I have not gone that route since (and that was over twenty years ago).

So many times we do things to be seen of men and we forget all about God. We have it all wrong! We are dressing upside-down! Say what? With *hemlines up and necklines down*, we become a distraction! Hemlines should be down, and necklines should be up. A physician (female) once said, "When we go shopping for our clothing, we only look at ourselves facing the front and sides; but we never look at the back"—to see just how we look to the public. Yes, it is about what "I want to wear and I don't care what anyone says"…right? We *do* care about what others think of our appearance, because we want them to tell us that we look good—but not when we do *not* look good. When we are told by someone that something does not look good on us, right away that person becomes a "hater" or is considered to be "jealous." We have to realize that not all fashions are designed for all shapes and sizes. We have to realize that just because "it is the design for the time," it was not necessarily designed with each of us in mind.

Sisters, God made us in His image and His likeness. We are all uniquely created for our own individuality—personality, beauty, physical structure, etc. We do not have to keep up with the Joneses, and it could very well be the case that the Joneses want to keep up with us. "Examine yourselves, whether ye be in the faith; prove your own selves. Know ye not your own selves, how that Jesus Christ is in you, except ye be reprobates *(morally depraved; unprincipled; bad; rejected by God and beyond hope of salvation)*?" (2 Corinthians 13:5).

Having been made in God's image, there is nothing wrong with the way we are shaped; after all, we were created in God's image and likeness. A friend of mine once gave me a gift after we finished a challenge of weight loss together. It was a plaque that was made out of ceramic, and it was round and brandished the words, "Round is a shape, too!" I thought that that was so great…because *I* am kind of "round." No matter what our shape is, we do not have to advertise it in such a way that everyone needs to see where the Bs (bulges) are. Our clothing should be a covering for us, not our skin. God took care of the skin "in the beginning."

And concerning the issue of being seen by others, sisters are very hard on each other. We sit back and sneer, talk about, and tease others behind their backs, though we have not even checked out our own backsides. We talk about the "skimpy clothing" that slender women wear, but we want to wear it, too—so we buy body briefers and undergarments that we think will hold it all in, and then pass out because of lack of circulation and an inability to breathe. Why should we wear something that we are not comfortable in? And just how is it that we know when others are uncomfortable in their clothing? Because when those persons come into the presence of others, right away, they start pulling up to cover the cleavage, and pull down in order to cover up the posterior.

Case in point, leggings are not for everyone (or for everywhere). As a matter of fact, such clothing is just getting us closer to being in the nude (naked). And if they are stretched enough, they can become see-through…and why would we want to show off what we have or do not have? We should leave some things to the imagination; trust me, doing so will get us a lot farther—and then, too, I guess it all depends on where we are planning to go. We can be proud people without putting ourselves on display. We must be modest for ourselves. The fashion industry has a team that works purposefully to design specific clothing lines that will make "them" money— because they know that someone will buy their goods (at any cost) just to be able to say that they "have" the latest thing…no matter how it looks. We must understand that not all designs are meant for everyone.

Think of the attire required for employment, school, business, church, special occasions, and so forth. Some people may actually wonder why they did not get hired, or why they were turned away at a five-star restaurant or a wedding reception. Wearing the proper attire and adhering to dress codes are important things to do for any occasion. When attending church services, we all should dress in modest apparel that puts us closer to holiness—that way, all attention can be directed toward the Lord (which is where it should be). The way we dress sends a message. We are not God and we do not know the content of one's heart, so we seek to draw conclusions from his or her appearance. Of course, one should be able to dress as he or she pleases; after all, "we live in America, the land of the free and the home of the brave"—right? Unfortunately, the way we dress stereotypes us into certain categories. This sentiment is detailed in 1 Timothy 2:9-10: "In like manner also, that women adorn themselves in *modest apparel*, with shamefacedness and sobriety; not with broided hair, or gold, or pearls, or costly array; But (which becometh women professing godliness) with good works." God, who provided this dress code, expects us as Christians to be obedient to these guidelines.

Sisters, how do we see ourselves? What are our names? What do we answer to? I ask these questions in considering the language we use to address each other. Why does anyone present himself or herself as a "garden tool"? Often, a girl, a young lady, or a woman is referred to as a "garden tool" ("hoe"), which is a shorter version of the term *whore* and means "a woman who engages in promiscuous sexual intercourse, usually, but not always, for money; prostitute; harlot; strumpet"; or she is called the "B" word, which is "a female dog; a malicious, unpleasant, selfish person, especially a woman; an obscene, indecent woman" (*the slang term* for this is "a person who performs demeaning tasks for another; servant: a convict who is in a homosexual relationship and/or domineering relationship willingly or unwillingly in the prison setting"). Since my mother did not give me any of these names, I should not answer to any degrading and disrespectful terms. They are not terms of endearment but, instead, are terms of degradation, bestowed upon individuals for their outward appearance (in mankind's eyes), or because they are so desperate for the attention of the opposite sex that they accept anything. And a person who gets involved with someone who has resorted to calling him or her names will eventually get tired of that name and expect a change. I once heard a man say, "Whatever you do or did to get that man or woman (gentlemen), it is going to take the same thing to keep him/her." Are we to think that that man will not use this logic: "That's what you answered to when I met you, so what is the problem now"? Sisters, ladies, we must not start something that we cannot finish—so we should not get into a relationship with someone who does not value us the way that God does.

~Hey, I'm just a "sista" tryin' to tell somebody about JESUS.~

    Brothers... I need help when it comes to trying to understand the appeal of the trend of "sagging." Thinking of sagging makes me think of a baby with a dirty diaper on. That is the visual that comes to my mind, which is not a pretty image when considering a male over the age of three years. Where did it come from? Help a "sister" out! Our men should understand that having sagging pants is not to be confused with having "swag" (although I am sure that there are some men who think that their sagging helps give them "swag").

    In researching this issue, statements were made that concerning incarcerated males, it is a trend for one male to wear his pants this way in order to identify himself as being available for sexual encounters with other males. STRIKE ONE! "And likewise also the men, leaving the natural use of the woman, burned in their lust one toward another; men with men working that which is unseemly, and receiving in themselves that recompence of their error which was meet" (Romans 1:27). The words of this Scripture verse provide the first reason for one's not wearing his pants that way. One minister has said this: "Brothers, pull your pants up! Don't nobody want to see what color your drawers are or how dirty they are." That sounds nasty, doesn't it? Well, it *is* nasty.

    In listening to a police interview about having encounters with persons wearing this kind of attire, it was said that police officers love it because when they are chasing suspects who are sagging, those persons cannot run, making it easier to apprehend them. Any person who is guilty of carrying himself that way should fix himself up, man up, and be a person of character! It is said that "birds of a feather flock together"; this means that while there are some young men and boys who might not be like that, their having association with or looking like people who "are like that" will get them stereotyped into the same category. Whatever happened to wearing shirts, sweaters, and casual slacks? Again, the fashion industry is of course really happy about males sporting this type of attire because it is making the money that those males could be saving. Everyone is expected to dress appropriately at all times—*including* the brothers. Whatever the occasion calls for is how one should dress. Everyone should be his own trendsetter—being a leader who guides others in the right direction instead of a follower being led in the wrong direction.

I ask the brothers these things: "How do you see yourselves? What are your names? What do you answer to? Did your mothers name you 'dog' or the N word?" I say this to the brothers: "You know the N word was buried in July of 2007, yet you still continue to abuse yourselves with such degradation, just as the woman allows herself to be called a B or a H." It appears that speaking slang is more important than speaking correct English; for a while, slang was considered "Ebonics." I say this to the brothers: "You are so gifted that you can come up with such clichés and label them as 'Ebonics'—which may sound like something good but, really, it 'separates the men from the boys'…and by engaging in such behavior, you choose to remain in the pits of slavery to what another chooses to label you. You could be the ones heading modern technology, yet you choose to stand on the street corners and do nothing. You could be the men in surgery—not having it, but *performing* it. I encourage you to man up and be the men that God has created you to be. Be the men to your brothers, fathers to your children, and husbands to your wives. As Christians, you are representing Christ…and not just in church, but everywhere you go: 'Let all things be done decently and in order' (1 Corinthians 14:40)."

~Hey, I'm just a "sista" tryin' to tell somebody about JESUS.~

My brothers and sisters, I encourage all of us to become more diligent in seeking what God has for our lives. In doing this, we are to assess things like the following: remember commandment #2 from the Ten Commandments (as discussed in chapter 3 of this book)? "Ye shall not make any cuttings in your flesh for the dead, nor print any marks upon you: I am the LORD" (Leviticus 19:28). While getting tattooed is a fad, it should not be. Okay, so one may have gotten one or more tattoos before he or she came into a relationship with the Lord—but now that he or she knows that tattoos are not pleasing to God, he or she should leave them alone and not add any more of them to his or her body. And those who do not want to get God involved in this decision should at least heed His warnings—for the sake of not catching the many strains of Hepatitis A, B, and C. It is not something that anyone would want in his or her body: "If my people, which are called by my name, shall humble themselves, and pray, and seek my face, and turn from their wicked ways; then will I hear from heaven, and will forgive their sin, and will heal their land" (2 Chronicles 7:14); "Abstain from all appearance of evil" (1 Thessalonians 5:22).

God wants us to treat our bodies as the temples He designed them to be: "I beseech you therefore, brethren, by the mercies of God, that ye present your bodies a living sacrifice, holy, acceptable unto God, which is your reasonable service. And be not conformed to this world: but be ye transformed by the renewing of your mind, that ye may prove what is that good, and acceptable, and perfect, will of God" (Romans 12:1-2); "Know ye not that your bodies are the members of Christ? ... What? know ye not that your body is the temple of the Holy Ghost which is in you, which ye have of God, and ye are not your own?" (1 Corinthians 6:15a, 19). Our bodies are temporary holding spaces for our souls until we leave this Earth. When we die, our bodies go back to dust and our souls go back to God. What more can be said concerning our bodies—what we put on them, what we do to them, and what we do in them?

~Hey, I'm just a "sista" tryin' to tell somebody about JESUS.~

Chapter 11

Teachers—Teaching about Marriage

*And Adam gave names to all cattle, and to the fowl of the air, and to every beast of the field; but for Adam there was not found an help meet for him. And the L*ord *God caused a deep sleep to fall upon Adam and he slept: and he took one of his ribs, and closed up the flesh instead thereof; And the rib, which the L*ord *God had taken from man, made he a woman, and brought her unto the man. And Adam said, This is now bone of my bones, and flesh of my flesh: she shall be called Woman, because she was taken out of Man. Therefore shall a man leave his father and his mother, and shall cleave unto his wife: and they shall be one flesh. And they were both naked, the man and his wife, and were not ashamed.—Genesis 2:20-25*

Marriage was designed by God for the purpose of "being fruitful and multiplying"...replenishing the Earth. God created one male and one female—that all the nations/descendants from that first "man" (Adam) and that first "woman" (Eve) would come.

In today's society, there is much controversy surrounding the subject of marriage: who should marry whom, and who should *not* marry. This will be brief (or, at least, it is my intent for it to be brief). As the above Scripture from the book of Genesis notes, marriage is assuredly to be between male and female. According to Scripture, it was not intended to be between two men or two women. This is detailed in the New Testament: "But from the beginning of the creation God made them *male and female*. For this cause shall a *man* leave his father and mother, and cleave to his *wife*; And they twain shall be one flesh: so then they are no more twain, but one flesh" (Mark 10:6-8); "Nevertheless let every one of you in particular so love his wife even as himself; and the wife see that she reverence her husband" (Ephesians 5:33). Notice these instructions: the man is to love *his* wife, and the wife is to reverence *her* husband—masculine *and* feminine genders.

To reiterate, "God blessed them, and God said unto them, Be fruitful, and multiply, and replenish the earth, and subdue it: and have dominion over the fish of the sea, and over the fowl of the air, and over every living thing that moveth upon the earth" (Genesis 1:28). Have we (humankind) so conformed to this world and become so contrary to the Word of God that we can do things our way and *live*? God requires our obedience to His Word and to His way. Although two plus two equals four, man plus man equals zero, and woman plus woman equals zero. (Remember the command in the Garden of Eden to the *man* and the *woman* to be fruitful [reproduce] and multiply [increase the number] and replenish [to make full or complete again] the Earth?)

Humankind has strayed so far from Scripture—so far from what God's plan is—that they are altering God's Word in order to accommodate them in the sin that they wallow in: "Professing themselves to be wise, they became fools, ... And even as they did not like to retain God in their knowledge, God gave them over to a reprobate mind, to do those things which are not convenient" (Romans 1:22, 28). (The word *reprobate* refers to "a depraved, unprincipled, or wicked person: a drunken reprobate; a person rejected by God and beyond hope of salvation; morally depraved [adjective]"; read Romans 1 to really get the full understanding.)

So why is this chapter even necessary? Because God wants us to understand that He is a forgiving God—and that it is necessary for those who choose to practice "alternative" lifestyles to seek God for deliverance. It has become a trend to be tolerant of same-sex marriages—and this "tolerance" has brought about the desire to change the Constitution (in ways that challenge the government) so that individual states around the country can change their laws to accommodate such behavior…because laws that hinder such have become offensive to many and are considered to be discrimination. What about me? I am offended that the lawmakers want to deviate from "what thus saith the Lord." Help us, Holy Ghost, in the name of Jesus!

~Hey, I'm just a "sista" tryin' to tell somebody about JESUS.~

Chapter 12

Conclusion

I beseech you therefore, brethren, by the mercies of God, that ye present your bodies a living sacrifice, holy, acceptable unto God, which is your reasonable service. And be not conformed to this world: but be ye transformed by the renewing of your mind, that ye may prove what is that good, and acceptable, and perfect, will of God.—Romans 12:1-2

There is not too much more that can be said here. This writing was to tell somebody about Jesus—and though the surface has not nearly been touched concerning Him, it is a brief starter for one to acquire the desire to learn of Him…to come to know Him for himself or herself. Paul wrote the following in Romans 10:1-3: "Brethren, my heart's desire and prayer to God for Israel is, that they might be saved. For I bear them record that they have a zeal of God, but not according to knowledge. For they being ignorant of God's righteousness, and going about to establish their own righteousness, have not submitted themselves unto the righteousness of God."

God grants us wisdom through Him: "If any of you lack wisdom, let him ask of God, that giveth to all men liberally, and upbraideth (criticize severely) not; and it shall be given him" (James 1:5). We cannot go against God or His Word: "There is no wisdom nor understanding nor counsel against the LORD" (Proverbs 21:30); "For we can do nothing against the truth, but for the truth" (2 Corinthians 13:8). Without God, we are a confused people refusing to be obedient to our Creator—and in regard to being disobedient, there is nothing more that can be said other than what was said in the beginning of this writing: "My people are destroyed for lack of knowledge: because thou hast rejected knowledge, I will also reject thee, that thou shalt be no priest to me: seeing thou hast forgotten the law of thy God, I will also forget thy children" (Hosea 4:6).

A very prominent minister—who has gone to be with the Lord—once said this of his ministry: "I felt it necessary to ring the fire bell in defense of the Word of God." My thought today is that *I am* ringing the fire bell as a warning. We want the Word to fit our circumstances instead of our conforming to God's Word. We cannot change it—as in taking away from God's Word or adding to it: "For I testify unto every man that heareth the words of the prophecy of this book, If any man shall add unto these things, God shall add unto him the plagues that are written in this book: And if any man shall take away from the words of the book of this prophecy, God shall take away his part out of the book of life, and out of the holy city, and from the things which are written in this book" (Revelation 22:18-19).

May God forever bless YOU according to His will—and may He prepare you for His will.

~Hey, I'm just a "sista" tryin' to tell somebody about JESUS.~

About the Author

Wilma Louise McGee has often said that "she was a princess born among four princes," because she was born into a family consisting of five children (and also having a father and mother and)—she being the only female child. She was born and raised in a Christian environment in Port Huron, Michigan. She hailed from a family of Kings, as she often puts it: her grandfather, her father, and one of her brothers were all named "King"—and, above all, "the KING": Jesus Christ. She accepted Christ at the age of twelve, because she loved to sing, hoping to become a member of her church choir (not knowing that she had to be fourteen years old before she could join). She started singing at the age of five, and her first solo was, "All Night, All Day, the Angels Watching over Me"—which has, of late, become one of the songs that she is most known for singing.

She professes that the beginning of her walk with the Lord was on Palm Sunday—in 1990—when "salvation came to her house" as she was singing the song, "Lead Me to Calvary." She says that God led her to the Cross...where Jesus died not only for "her" sins, but also for the sins of the whole world.

Wilma began writing probably around the age of twenty-three, soon after her son was born. She would write poems or just write about what was on her mind at the time, or about what she saw. For example, she spent a lot of time at Belle Isle, an island park in Detroit, Michigan; there, she would park her car along the water, or sit on a blanket on the ground, at a picnic table, or on a rock by the water, and watch the water flow—which sometimes would move briskly and, at other times, would just be still. There, too, she would listen to the sounds around her: the wind blowing, birds singing, the water beating against the shoreline, and children and families enjoying themselves on the summer days (or even in the winter). Sometimes she would watch the deer and other animals hunt for food and, on occasion, would get out of her car and make a snow angel herself; but, mostly she would listen and write to God, telling Him about the things she saw, her thoughts, and her desires, giving Him thanks for His goodness shown toward her and her son, and reading His Word—as in 2 Timothy 3:16: "All scripture is given by inspiration of God, and is profitable for doctrine, for reproof, for correction, for instruction in righteousness." She would wait for a word from the Lord.

Writing became something that Wilma enjoyed doing over time, and she found that her writings were most interesting when reread sometime later…like days, months, even years into the future. She often says, "To God be the glory" for the things He has done in her life, for the things He is doing in her life, and for the things He is about to do in her life.

~HEY! I'M JUST A "SISTA" TRYIN' TO TELL SOMEBODY ABOUT JESUS!~

NOTES

NOTES

NOTES

NOTES

NOTES

NOTES

www.ingramcontent.com/pod-product-compliance
Lightning Source LLC
Chambersburg PA
CBHW052029290426
44112CB00014B/2437